Teaching for Results

Other Titles of Interest by Rowman & Littlefield Education

*Supervising Student Teachers:
The Professional Way*, 7th Edition
By Marvin A. Henry and Ann Weber

*A Complete Guide to Rubrics Assessment
Made Easy for Teachers*, 2nd Edition
By Audrey M. Quinlan

*Dynamic Educational Leadership Teams:
From Mine to Ours*
By Matthew Jennings

*Team-Based Professional Development:
A Process for School Reform*
By Judith T. Witmer and Steven A. Melnick

*Differentiating Instruction for At-Risk Students:
What to Do and How to Do It*
By Rita Dunn and Andrea Honigsfeld

*Creative Adventures in Social Studies:
Engaging Activities & Essential
Questions to Inspire Students*
By Daniel R. Peppercorn

Teaching for Results

Best Practices in Integrating Co-Teaching and Differentiated Instruction

Matthew J. Jennings

ROWMAN & LITTLEFIELD EDUCATION

A division of
ROWMAN & LITTLEFIELD PUBLISHERS, INC.
Lanham • New York • Toronto • Plymouth, UK

Published by Rowman & Littlefield Education
A division of Rowman & Littlefield Publishers, Inc.
A wholly owned subsidiary of The Rowman & Littlefield Publishing Group, Inc.
4501 Forbes Boulevard, Suite 200, Lanham, Maryland 20706
www.rowman.com

10 Thornbury Road, Plymouth PL6 7PP, United Kingdom

Copyright © 2012 by Matthew J. Jennings

All rights reserved. No part of this book may be reproduced in any form or by any electronic or mechanical means, including information storage and retrieval systems, without written permission from the publisher, except by a reviewer who may quote passages in a review.

British Library Cataloguing in Publication Information Available

Library of Congress Cataloging-in-Publication Data
Jennings, Matthew.
  Teaching for results : best practices in integrating co-teaching and differentiated instruction / Matthew J. Jennings.
     p. cm.
  Includes bibliographical references.
  ISBN 978-1-61048-783-2 (pbk.)—ISBN 978-1-61048-784-9 (electronic)
 1. Teaching teams. 2. Individualized instruction. 3. Lesson planning. 4. Classroom management. 5. Mixed ability grouping in education. I. Title.

LB1029.T4J46 2012
371.2'52—dc23
                                                                    2012020133

Contents

1. Integrating Co-Teaching and Differentiated Instruction — 1
2. Team Development — 11
3. Laying the Foundation for a Collaborative Classroom — 23
4. Assessment for and of Learning — 41
5. Instructional Planning and Preparation — 57
6. Instruction in a Co-Taught Classroom — 77
7. Continuous Improvement — 89
8. The Role of the Administration — 97

Appendix — 111

References — 117

About the Author — 119

CHAPTER 1

Integrating Co-Teaching and Differentiated Instruction

Imagine two elementary school classrooms, both consisting of twenty-three students and two full-time teachers. Of the twenty-three students, six of them are identified for receiving special education services via an in-class support model. One of the teachers is a general education teacher and the other is certified to teach special education. Unfortunately, this is where the similarities end.

When observing in classroom A you notice that both of these teachers move freely about the classroom, sharing one another's resources and materials. Furthermore, it is difficult to tell which of the students have disabilities, because they are all dispersed evenly throughout the classroom.

It is also difficult to tell which of the two teachers is the general education teacher. Their communication is open and honest, representing the positive models of adult collaboration some of their students desperately need to witness. Both of the teachers are actively engaged in the entire presentation of the lesson, switching roles seamlessly. Students address their questions and discussion points to both of the teachers. The few minor discipline issues noted are handled by the teacher in closest proximity to the offending student.

As you look at the plans left out on the desk, you realize that a great deal of thought has gone into planning the lesson you are seeing. The teachers have successfully differentiated the concepts all students must learn from those things only some students need to know. Furthermore, you can easily see how the differentiated goals have been used to make accommodations in the content and activities of the lesson. At the end of your observation, you leave feeling that these students are very fortunate to be having this experience with these teachers.

After driving across town to a different elementary school in the same school district you enter classroom B. Almost immediately you get a very different feeling from this classroom. The clear labeling of materials with the teachers' names gives you the distinct impression that these teachers have been forced to share the space. Even more troubling is the fact that the students with disabilities are seated together in close proximity to the special education teacher's desk.

It is easy to determine who the "real teacher" is in this classroom. She leads the entire whole-group part of the lesson while the other teacher moves in and out of the student desks, reminding students to stay on task. When it comes time to break into small groups for additional practice, the special education teacher and the six students identified for special education services go to their table in the back of the classroom. At this table, the special education teacher works with "her students" on content that has no apparent connection to the whole-class material just presented.

Contrary to the planning observed in classroom A, you notice no substantive difference between the plans in classroom B and those you would see in the other general education classrooms. Besides listing the required individualized educational plan (IEP) modifications, there is no evidence of differentiating the processes or products used in this lesson. You leave this observation feeling sad for the students and angry with the teachers.

How is it possible for two classrooms with the identified similarities to produce such different results? Is it simply the natural chemistry the teachers in class A have? Is it a lack of willingness by the teachers in class B to put forth the time and effort required to succeed? In fact, both of these variables may have played a part in the development of these teams. However, typically they would not account for the vast majority of the differences observed.

Collaborative teaching is a set of skills that can be learned. More specifically, with sufficient effort, at least a moderate level of collaborative skills, and a positive attitude, any pair of certified teachers can learn how to successfully operate in a collaboratively taught classroom.

Frequently extrinsic reasons are given by both teachers and administrators for the lack of success with collaborative teaching. A lack of common planning time and quality professional development are the two most frequently cited reasons for this situation.

Without a doubt school administrators can provide conditions in schools that make it easier for co-teaching to thrive. In fact, the final chapter of this book will address this topic. However, the primary purpose of this book is to provide co-teachers with knowledge and skills they can use to improve the aspects of collaborative teaching that they control.

In particular, this book will address how two teachers can build a positive working relationship that they then can use to co-manage, co-assess, co-plan, and co-instruct a group of diverse learners in any subject area at any grade level. However, prior to addressing these topics, it is essential to be clear regarding the type of co-teaching the information in this book is intended to be applied towards.

DEFINING CO-TEACHING

For the purposes of this book, co-teaching is defined as the partnership between two or more *certified professionals* for the co-managing, co-planning, co-instructing, and co-assessing of a group of students with diverse needs in the same general education classroom. To further comprehend this definition, it is important to note specific elements that have been excluded. For example, co-teaching is not a teacher working with a paraprofessional. Unless that paraprofessional has the knowledge and skills expected of a certified teacher, it is unrealistic to expect them to co-manage, co-plan, co-instruct, or co-assess in the manner described throughout this book.

Collaborative teaching is not occurring when the students with disabilities are regularly pulled from the classroom to work with one of the professionals. Collaborative teaching is also not occurring when a group of students with disabilities is consistently instructed in a separate part of the general education classroom. Separating students from the classroom setting as part of meeting identified needs is appropriate. However, it should not be regular and it should not be based upon eligibility labels.

Purposefully excluded from the definition provided at the beginning of this section is any reference to the teachers being equals. To state that both partners should be equals in the partnership ignores the fact that these teachers usually bring different knowledge bases and skill sets to the partnership. In the case of the general education teacher, it is commonly strong knowledge of the curriculum and experience with content-related instructional strategies.

For the support teacher, whether it is special education, basic skills, or English as a second language, it is knowledge of how to improve access to that content via individualized strategies. It is unrealistic and likely ineffective to expect a special education teacher without the background in a subject area to act as an equal instructor or assessor of that content. It is equally ludicrous to expect the typical subject area teacher to substantially modify assignments.

Over time, teachers working effectively in collaborative teaching situations will develop new knowledge and skills. In fact, the job-embedded professional development possible when teaching collaboratively is one of the major strengths of this instructional model. However in the vast majority of situations, the initial goal must be to make sure both individuals maximize the use of their knowledge, skills, and talents to substantively improve the quality of instruction provided in the classroom.

Lastly, co-teaching is not a marriage. That analogy is both overused and inaccurate. First, in most Western civilizations marriage is entered into voluntarily with partners selecting one another. Collaborative teaching partners are frequently assigned whom they will work with. Second, in marriage the partners can decide to separate. Collaborative teaching partners are together in their partnership for as long as the school administration decides to keep them that way. In some ways a co-teaching relationship is more restrictive than a marriage!

WHY CO-TEACH?

Obviously co-teaching is used as a method for meeting the least restrictive environment requirements found in the Individuals with Disabilities Educational Improvement Act. It is also used in secondary settings to meet the No Child Left Behind Act's requirement that the teacher of record must possess a teaching credential in that content area. While these may be the mandated reasons, most teachers do not find them to be the most motivating or meaningful ones.

Every teacher I have met entered the profession with the hope of making a difference in the lives of their students. It is inevitable that every teacher in the profession who has taught for an extended period of time will be confronted with students they are unable to successfully instruct. For those that care deeply about the results of their efforts, this can be a very disconcerting experience. Because educators typically work in isolation, they have no one who truly understands their situation with whom they can engage in problem-solving activities.

Colleagues sharing classroom instruction have a common frame of reference. This creates the potential for enhanced problem-solving through the sharing of diverse perspectives. In other words, joint problem-solving by co-teaching pairs typically leads to better results, and better results lead to enhanced motivation.

It has been said that the only thing teachers working in the same school building must share is the parking lot. Some teachers like it this way. However, most teachers experience various degrees of feeling isolated. This makes sense considering the fact that teachers spend the vast majority of their professional time working with children. Having a collaborative teaching partner decreases feelings of isolation.

Teaching is challenging work. Often you do not know the results of your efforts until long after your instruction is completed. Every teacher that engages in reflection upon their work will have moments of self-doubt. Some struggling teachers may be fortunate enough to get sympathetic ears from loved ones, but unless they have experienced the struggles for themselves those loved ones truly can't understand the experience. However, having a collaborative teaching partner who is experiencing the same situation has the potential to increase feelings of interpersonal support.

Teachers that plan together and then share instruction have a tremendous opportunity to learn from one another. Special education teachers can develop increased knowledge of content and subject-specific instructional strategies. General education teachers have the opportunity to increase their ability to individualize instruction. Add structured opportunities for reflection and collaborative teaching offers one of the most powerful opportunities for personal and professional development.

Whenever I do a workshop on the topic of collaborative teaching, I ask audience members to share with me other benefits resulting from having a collaborative teaching partner. Inevitably their list is far more practical than mine. Teachers frequently cite the fact that having two teachers in the class allows them to spend less time on direct behavior management. Having two teachers that effectively use classroom space allows for increased physical proximity between teacher and students. If you don't believe that physical proximity plays a major role in encouraging socially acceptable behavior, than ask yourself what you did the last time you saw a police car in your rearview mirror.

Another practical benefit frequently cited is continuity of instruction when an absence from school is required. Rather than face the chaos of returning to school after being absent, some teachers will choose to come to work ill. Having a co-teaching partner provides the peace of mind that someone knowledgeable about the classroom routine and students will be in that class. When needed, an absence does not result in more work than it is worth.

Teachers should be written up in medical journals for the size and elasticity of their bladders. A teacher working solo in a classroom cannot leave that classroom unattended to deal with "personal needs." This can be for very long blocks of time. With a co-teaching partner present, a teacher can temporarily leave the classroom to do whatever may be necessary.

Unfortunately, today many parents accept the statements made by their children over the word of the teacher. Living in a very litigious society, it has become increasingly valuable to have a "second set of eyes" in the classroom. When a difficult situation arises, another adult is present, serving as a witness to the classroom activities.

Thus, there are many potential benefits for the adults working in a collaborative teaching situation. What about the students? When done appropriately, with the appropriate level of supports and services, collaborative teaching provides tremendous benefits to both general and special education students.

One of the most common complaints school staff members hear when collaborative teaching is introduced comes from the parents of general education students. These parents typically object to having their child placed in a classroom with special education students because they believe it will result in decreased academic achievement for their child. In fact, most of the research in this area cites a neutral to positive gain for all students in collaboratively taught classrooms (Sharpe, York, & Knight 1994; Hunt, Staub, Alwell, & Goetz, 1994; Hollowood, Salisbury, Rainforth, & Palombaro, 1995). Of course, this would not be the case in a classroom where collaborative instruction is not being done according to research-based principles. Yet the same could be said for a classroom taught by one teacher.

It is unfortunate that some of our students are not exposed to positive models of adult collaboration. Children growing up in homes where adult relationships are dysfunctional do not get exposure to what positive adult collaboration can look like. Poor real-life models are only further reinforced by the fascination television has with portraying dysfunctional adult relationships. It may be the case that the relationship modeled between two teachers in a collaboratively taught classroom is the only exposure these students have to positive models of adult collaboration.

When mainstreaming was popular, groups of students from self-contained classrooms would join their peers for activities like lunch or special subject area activities. Inevitably school staff members would conclude that mainstreaming was not promoting the social integration desired. In retrospect this should serve as no surprise.

One of the most important predictors of who forms friendships is physical proximity. Think about the first close friendship you ever developed. Chances are it was someone that you lived near or spent a lot of time with. Students from a self-contained special education classroom formed relationships with other students from that self-contained classroom. Simply putting them with other students for a small portion of the day was not going change whom they had grown comfortable with. If we want to create more inclusive school cultures then we need to integrate students for a larger part of the school day.

In addition to increasing the chances positive relationships will develop among all of our students, placement in collaboratively taught classrooms also provides students with disabilities that impact their social functioning potential models of age-appropriate social skills and behaviors.

In some cases positive models are insufficient for changing student behavior. Just like students need direct instruction in math or reading, some students will require direct instruction in social skills. However, even in these cases, placement in a general education classroom will provide the opportunity for transfer and generalization of learned skills to a more authentic context. For the general education students, working with students that have special needs provides the opportunity for them to learn tolerance of differences.

When we label a child, there is a strong tendency for that child to demonstrate behaviors characteristic of that label. In other words, tell students they have a learning disability and they are more likely to act like students with a learning disability. Furthermore, believing oneself to be disabled is bound to result in the lowering of one's self concept. Wouldn't it be better if we could provide the services required to all of our students without having to label them?

With collaborative teaching this is possible. In a collaboratively taught classroom educators are bringing the services to the students without requiring students to have a label to receive services. When two teachers are working effectively in a collaboratively taught classroom, they are both using their knowledge and skills to help all of the students.

A special education teacher in an effective co-taught classroom will use his or her knowledge to assist any child in that class regardless of whether they qualify for an individualized educational program. No more will the children in that classroom not receive the assistance they need simply because there was not enough of a discrepancy between their IQ score and their achievement.

INTEGRATING DIFFERENTIATED INSTRUCTION

Collaborative teaching is a not an instructional strategy. It is a structure through which teachers can work collaboratively to deliver instruction. Due to the diverse nature of a co-taught classroom, it is essential for this instruction to be differentiated to meet a wide variety of students' needs.

Differentiating instruction can be challenging, even for master teachers. To differentiate instruction effectively requires strong classroom management skills, the ability to effectively employ a wide variety of instructional strategies, and the ability to administer and interpret valid assessments.

If a teacher cannot manage the classroom, having students engaged in multiple activities will be chaotic. If a teacher does not have mastery over a variety of instructional strategies then they will not be able to effectively deliver differentiated activities. If the teacher cannot administer and interpret assessments they will not be able to provide valid information about students' needs and interests.

In addition to requiring high levels of classroom-specific skills, providing differentiated instruction requires hard work. However, it is definitely reasonable to expect differentiated instruction when there are two instructors in the classroom pooling their knowledge and sharing the responsibilities.

The remainder of this book will describe a clear means for providing differentiated instructional practices through the co-teaching model. More specifically, the content of these chapters will provide readers with a practical understanding of what collaborative teaching should look like in the classroom and how co-teaching as an instructional model can make differentiated instruction more effective and realistic. In the next chapter readers will learn about the developmental nature of a co-teaching relationship. Successful teamwork is the foundation for achieving the benefits of co-teaching.

Points to Remember

- Successful collaborative teaching requires a set of skills, which can be learned.
- Co-teaching is the partnership between two or more certified professionals for the co-managing, co-planning, co-instructing, and co-assessing of a group of students with diverse needs in the same general education classroom.

- When done with the appropriate level of supports and services, co-teaching has many potential benefits for both teachers and students.
- Co-teaching is an organizational structure that makes differentiating instruction feasible.

CHAPTER 2

Team Development

While collaborative teaching is not analogous to marriage, it is certainly a relationship. Like most relationships, if it is dysfunctional it will have negative consequences for those involved. In this situation a dysfunctional relationship will result in teachers not effectively using their knowledge and skills to meet the needs of their students. Clearly this is not acceptable.

Often two teachers are assigned to work with one another and are simply expected to "make it work." Sometimes they do and sometimes they don't. Considering the importance of the quality of this teaming, this is not something that should be left to chance.

The development of a collaborative teaching team is a process. Like all groups, a collaborative teaching team will progress through a series of predictable developmental stages. Teams will not progress through these stages at the same rate, nor will every team successfully transition from one stage to the next. Some teams will get stuck in one of the stages, while others will progress to the final stage rapidly. However, most teams will experience most of the characteristics associated with each of the three stages described below.

Understanding that the teamwork dimension of collaborative teaching is a developmental process is typically met with a sense of relief by the teachers involved. Knowing that it takes time for this relationship to develop makes it possible to accept the realities and challenges of each stage in the progression.

A COMMON, COMPELLING PURPOSE

Progressing from stage one of collaborative teaching to stage three requires effort and commitment. In order to spark and sustain the necessary motivation, it is important at the onset for team members to develop a common and compelling purpose. This common and compelling purpose is a future state of affairs desired enough by both teachers to motivate them to collectively apply their skills and knowledge in order to work toward its achievement. This purpose must be important and it must not be something either partner could achieve individually.

For a collaborative teaching team a common and compelling purpose is translated into action through a team goal. The following process will lead to setting, implementing, and evaluating a student achievement goal for a collaborative teaching team. The first step is the identification of students' current level of academic performance.

At the beginning of a school year, co-teaching partners must use some form of pre-assessment data to determine their students' current level of academic achievement. This data may come from previously administered standardized tests or from locally developed assessments. Regardless of the source of the data, co-teachers must be able to identify the areas of student need that are of the highest priority. The data for the area of need selected as most critical will serve as the baseline for eventually measuring progress toward the identified goal.

The following is an example of baseline data used for developing a goal statement. *In September, the results of administering the Dynamic Indicators of Basic Early Literacy Skills (DIBELS) showed that 12 of our students met the benchmark criteria. Three of our students met the criteria for strategic intervention, as they did not demonstrate proficiency in all four subtest areas. Two of our students met the criteria for intensive intervention, and are considered at risk for reading failure.*

Step two is the development of the team's goal statement. In order for this goal to be effective, it must meet the criteria for being "POWERful."

P—Positively Interdependent
O—Operational
W—Worthwhile
E—Explicit
R—Rational

A positively interdependent goal requires partners to be connected with one another in such a way that they cannot succeed unless they both succeed. Without positive interdependence there is little extrinsic reason for partners to collaboratively strive for goal attainment.

An operational goal is one for which the results can be both observed and counted. The operational aspect of the goal provides the feedback necessary for the co-teaching team to formatively and summatively assess its progress as it relates to successful goal attainment.

A worthwhile goal is one that the partners perceive to be both challenging and consequential. It is neither too easy to complete nor well beyond the current capabilities of the team. In addition, co-teaching partners perceive completion of the goal as being relevant to both their individual needs and the needs of their students. When partners view attainment of the goal as worthwhile, it energizes them to use higher levels of effort toward goal completion.

Explicit goals are clear and specific. Both partners know what the goal has been formulated to accomplish as well as how they will recognize when it has been achieved. An explicit goal has a clear deadline for completion. Establishing a realistic time frame by which the goal is to be completed keeps achievement of that goal a high priority for the co-teachers.

The last element of a "POWERful" goal is that the goal must be rational. A goal is considered rational when it is based on solid evidence. The impetus for selecting the goal must be based on solid reasons. What qualitative or quantitative evidence exists to justify the team's efforts toward achieving this goal? If there is no evidence to support the selection of the goal, then there is an increased probability that the goal will not achieve significant results.

After discussion and drafting, the partners can use the following questions to assess the quality of their goal statements.

- Could this goal be accomplished by either one of us alone?
- Will we know if the goal has been achieved?
- Is attainment of this goal important in our current situation?
- Would the goal be clear to a stranger reading it?
- Is there a specific deadline for achieving this goal?
- Is there evidence supporting the need for this goal?

If the answer to any of these questions is no, then the goal should be revised until the answer is yes. The following is a goal statement related to the baseline data cited above. *On the end-of-year administration of the DIBELS assessment, all of our students will score at the benchmark level.*

Step three of this goal-setting process is the development of a plan for meeting this goal. The content of the plan is the instructional strategies co-teaching team members will implement in order to reach their goal. In order to have a high probability of success these strategies should be research-based and appropriate for the subject matter as well as the maturity level of the students taught.

The following is a description of the strategies a collaborative teaching team might use to meet the goal established above. *As a team we will attend a two-day workshop training designed to teach us how to use the Wilson Fundations curriculum. We will implement this program with our whole class for 30 minutes daily. For the students identified as strategic or intensive, we will provide an additional 30 minutes of small group instruction three days per week. The two students identified as intensive will receive 20 additional minutes of one-on-one reading instruction during our guided reading group time.*

Throughout the time period spent co-teaching, it is important that the team formally monitors student progress toward goal completion through the ongoing use of formative assessments. When necessary the results of the formative assessments should lead to adjustments in instructional strategies. This is a cyclical process designed to ultimately lead to goal attainment.

Near the end of the school year the team must deliver a post-assessment designed to measure student growth toward the goal from the time when the pre-assessment occurred. The post-assessment data will serve to inform the co-teachers of the level of success they have achieved in meeting their goal. Table 2.1 is a completed example of the template co-teachers can use to structure and document the goal-setting process. A blank copy of this template is located in the appendix.

This process for developing, monitoring, and implementing a clear, compelling purpose will serve as the motivation collaborative teaching teams will need in order to progress through the stages of collaborative teaching.

Table 2.1. Goal-Setting Template

	Collaborative Teaching Team's Goal-Setting Template
Baseline Data	In September, the results of administering the Dynamic Indicators of Basic Early Literacy Skills (DIBELS) showed that twelve of our students met the benchmark criteria. Three of our students met the criteria for strategic intervention, as they did not demonstrate proficiency in all four subtest areas. Two of our students met the criteria for intensive intervention and are considered at risk for reading failure.
Goal Statement	On the end-of-year administration of the DIBELS assessment all of our students will score at the benchmark level.
Strategies	As a team we will attend a two-day workshop training designed to teach us how to use the Wilson Fundations curriculum. We will implement this program with our whole class for 30 minutes daily. For the students identified as strategic or intensive, we will provide an additional 30 minutes of small-group instruction three days per week. The two students identified as intensive will receive 20 additional minutes of one-on-one reading instruction during our guided reading group time.
Outcome	

STAGE ONE

The first stage in the progression can be described as the "getting to know you" phase. This phase is characterized by feelings of awkwardness. Because it is frequently their classroom to begin with, general education teachers may demonstrate possessiveness toward the physical space, the students, and the content of instruction. The co-teacher teachers may feel unimportant, excluded, and not in control of the situation. It is often described as feeling like being a guest in someone else's home. The general mentality exhibited by the co-teachers is one of "my kids, your kids." The communication between the teachers is characterized as superficial and polite with a heavy emphasis on avoiding areas of conflict.

At this stage in their development, the single most important goal for the co-teachers on this team is to build a foundation of trust. Trust is the base upon which all successful co-teaching relationships are built. More specifically, teachers that are members of a high-performing co-teaching team have a high level of confidence that their partner has positive and honorable intentions. Certain that their partner has a genuine desire to do what is best for them and their students, the teachers will not feel the need to be overly protective or cautious when working together.

As a result, partners will be willing to make themselves vulnerable to one another. In other words, they will have confidence that their respective vulnerabilities, including weaknesses, skill deficiencies, interpersonal shortcomings, mistakes, and requests for help, will not be used against them. Not concerned about protecting themselves, teachers will focus their energy on the task to be accomplished and not the management of appearances.

Trust is a dynamic aspect of the relationship between co-teaching partners. It will increase or decrease based upon the actions of each team member. Repeated actions that are considered trusting and trustworthy will lead to the establishment of high levels of trust between the partners.

Without interpersonal risk, trust will not develop among the partners of a collaborative teaching team. In other words, for trust to develop one of the partners has to risk being vulnerable and then see whether the other will abuse that vulnerability. Vulnerability in a co-teaching situation is exhibited when one of the partners demonstrates openness. This openness can be the sharing of information, ideas, thoughts, feelings, or reactions to the tasks the team is completing.

A display of openness can be met by either confirmation or rejection. Confirmation is displayed through the communication of high regard for the partner as well as his or her contributions to the completion of the task. Confirmation does not always equate to agreement. Through their language and actions partners can disagree with the content of one another's ideas while still demonstrating respect for each other.

Rejection is demonstrated when a member of the team uses ridicule or disrespect in response to the other's openness. Sarcasm, laughing at personal disclosures that are serious, moralizing about behavior, and remaining silent when a response would be appropriate are behaviors that can be perceived as demonstrating rejection. Once perceived, rejection will erode the trust within the partnership.

Even though it takes time to build trust, it is something that can be destroyed quickly and easily. One common example of an action that destroys trust between co-teachers is when one partner talks negatively about the other outside the boundaries of the team relationship. Even though it may be "venting," sharing frustrations or criticisms about your co-teaching partner outside of the collaborative team setting will be the end of any trust that has been established. Trust in a co-teaching partnership must be built, valued, and protected if the team is to succeed.

Unfortunately trust can be destroyed far more quickly than it can be built. The development of trust requires shared experiences over time, multiple instances of openness, and an in-depth understanding of the unique attributes of one's partner. However, by taking a focused approach a collaborative teaching team can accelerate the process, achieving trust faster than if left to chance.

Early in the relationship, it is vital for the partners to get to know one another on a personal level. It does not need to be a long, in-depth process, but the partners must begin seeing one another as human beings with interesting backgrounds and unique life stories. Seeing one another as more than just colleagues assigned to work together facilitates the development of empathy and understanding between the pair.

In a relatively short period of time, partners can take the first step toward building trust. For those that prefer informal activities and settings, it can be a "lunch date" in which the partners talk about each other's backgrounds and interests. For those that prefer structure, it can be taking turns sharing answers to a short list of questions. Examples of effective discussion questions include:

- What and where have you taught?
- How many siblings do you have?
- Where did you grow up?
- What do you do for fun when you have free time?
- What was your first teaching job?

Any questions that are not overly sensitive in nature and are about the individual would be appropriate for this activity. By describing these attributes and experiences, co-teaching partners will begin to relate to one another on a more personal level.

Another option that is more time consuming is the administration of a tool that identifies each partner's behavioral preferences and personality styles. One such tool is the Myers Briggs Type Indicator (MBTI). The purpose of the MBTI is to provide practical and scientifically valid behavioral descriptions of team members according to the diverse ways they think, speak, and act. Sharing this information with one another helps to break down barriers because it allows partners to better understand and empathize with each other. If possible, the MBTI should be administered and interpreted by someone with the appropriate training. This will avoid the misuse or misinterpretation of the results obtained.

STAGE TWO

The second stage in the progression can be described as the "my turn, your turn" stage. While the teachers in this stage do tend to decrease their territorial behavior, the division of responsibilities remains clearly defined. For example, the general education teacher may "give up" some aspect of the lesson (giving the spelling test, correcting the homework, etc.) to the support teacher. As a result, students will know that both adults in the classroom are teachers, but they will consider one the main teacher while the other will be viewed as a helper. The communication between the teachers increases and will be characterized by the presence of some degree of conflict.

This conflict can be either destructive or productive. To promote team development, it is important for the co-teaching partners to engage in conflict that is productive. Productive conflict occurs when the co-teaching partners discuss the advantages and disadvantages of proposed actions, with the intent to create novel solutions to problems of critical importance to their students and their classroom.

This type of conflict is not characterized by pride and competition between the partners. Neither are the partners trying to get their way, nor are they trying to win. Instead, team members engaged in this type of conflict are pursuing the best possible solution to any problem or dilemma.

Destructive conflict occurs when the discussions are personality-based attacks designed to be mean-spirited or hurtful. Destructive fighting and interpersonal attacks are never acceptable behaviors for members of a collaborative teaching team. Not only do these behaviors destroy trust, they also inhibit the free expression of support for ideas, as well as doubts and objections.

Once members of a co-teaching team learns to engage in productive conflict they will find that important issues will be discussed more thoroughly. Alternatives to a proposal or suggestion will be carefully considered from multiple viewpoints. As a result, the quality of the decisions will increase.

In addition, the collaborative teaching team will become more efficient. When a conflict is avoided in one setting, there is a tendency for that conflict to arise again in future settings. Important conflicts do not simply just disappear. Collaborative teaching teams that avoid conflict waste time because they tend to revisit issues repeatedly without ever achieving resolution. Not only is this inefficient, it is frustrating and tends to lower morale.

Collaborative teaching team members that avoid conflict often do so in a misguided attempt to promote harmony. This artificial harmony frequently results in a dangerous underlying tension among partners. When members of a team do not openly debate and disagree about important ideas, they often resort to private attacks in the staff lounge or parking lot. These back-channel attacks are far worse and more damaging than spirited conflict over issues of importance.

Collaborative teaching teams that embrace the need to engage in productive conflict consist of partners that force themselves to say everything that needs to be said when the time is appropriate. As a result there is nothing remaining that needs to be said behind closed doors.

Lastly, productive conflict in which partners believe their ideas have been thoughtfully and genuinely considered will result in increased member commitment to the implementation of decisions. Regardless of the outcome reached, most people who believe their opinions have been listened to will commit to seeing a decision through to completion.

Like trust, the ability to engage in productive conflict can be developed through several actions. The first step is for the partners to acknowledge the fact that conflict, while potentially uncomfortable, is necessary for the growth of the partnership. Beyond this recognition, partners can also employ several other simple methods for making conflict more acceptable and productive.

The first strategy is to change how conflict is viewed. Instead of viewing conflict as a win-lose situation, the co-teachers must strive to reframe conflicts as problem-solving opportunities. The perspective of conflict as an "it" rather than a "who" makes the conflict-related dialogue an opportunity for learning and growth.

Teams with high levels of trust among members can tolerate task-related conflict and use the conflict productively (Levi, 2007). While the development of interpersonal trust can be accelerated through the use of the strategies previously described, it will take time.

Until this necessary level of trust has been established, the co-teachers may need to assign themselves an advocacy position for alternative solutions to problems that are both important and solvable. For example, suppose the co-teachers need to decide if one of their students should be kept from attending a field trip due to poor classroom behavior. Regardless of their original position, one of the teachers takes the position for having the student attend the trip, while the other will take the position for having the student not participate. In turn, each partner advocates for their assigned point of view. This process increases the probability that the advantages and disadvantages of each option are thoughtfully considered.

STAGE THREE

The final stage in the continuum can be described as the "thinking as one" stage. In this stage, both teachers experience a high comfort level. Abundant humor, communication, and acceptance are evident. A casual observer would have a difficult time distinguishing the "main teacher" in the classroom. The overall mentality of the teachers at stage three in their development is "our class, our students."

In stage three collective commitments are made, mutual and individual accountability is developed, and the focus is on collective results. This is the point in the relationship where the focus has shifted away from personal concerns about team teaching toward the task of meeting the students' needs.

Collaborative teaching teams do not continue performing at high levels forever. Research on work teams suggests that after a few years they may reach a point where longevity no longer is a benefit to performance (Guzzo & Dickson, 1996). However, it is both disheartening to the partners and counterproductive to the organization when a stage-three collaborative teaching team is prematurely separated.

Due to the staffing constraints associated with small schools it may not be possible to keep collaborative teaching teams together from year to year. This fact is understandable. However, the more frequent reason for separating two successful collaborative teaching team members is the assumption they will "spread" the effectiveness to two new partners.

It is at this point that well-meaning school administrators must be reminded that collaborative teaching teams are not like viruses; they cannot be spread through contact. Even though their experience may be beneficial to their rate of progress with a new partner, new collaborative teaching teams will begin at stage one.

Keeping a stage-three collaborative teaching team together for an extended period of time will yield positive results for students and high levels of morale for co-teaching partners. If it is possible, it should be a high priority for the responsible administrator.

Points to Remember

- Co-teaching is a developmental process.
- Co-teaching teams need a "POWERful" goal to serve as their common and compelling purpose.
- Trust is the foundation of the co-teaching relationship.
- Unlike destructive conflict, productive conflict is essential for the growth and effectiveness of a co-teaching team.
- Co-teaching teams that perform at a high level should be kept together for an extended, but not indefinite, period of time.

CHAPTER 3

Laying the Foundation for a Collaborative Classroom

Teachers of a collaboratively taught classroom have unique advanced planning requirements that they must satisfy in order to meet the needs of their students. Unlike in a regular general education classroom, teachers in a co-teaching situation must meet the requirements described in each child's individualized education plan (IEP). Both teachers should review the contents of the IEP prior to or very soon after working with the students.

This can be accomplished in settings where teachers are not responsible for a vast number of students. When general education teachers have a large number of students with individualized educational plans it is important to provide them with the most critical information in a concise and accessible form. The following "summary form" provides a practical reference far more likely to be used by general education teachers than the entire IEP document.

This form should be completed by the child's case manager or a special education teacher. It can easily be done during or soon after the actual meeting held to create the IEP. Teachers must be told that these documents contain confidential information and thus should be kept in a secure location. A completed example is provided in table 3.1. A blank copy of this template is located in the appendix.

Another aspect of the IEP the teachers must be aware of is students' required related services. It is very frustrating to teachers and ineffective for students when related services are scheduled during critical instructional times. On the other hand, related service providers have to meet many students' needs within the time constraints of the school day. Being

Table 3.1. IEP Summary Sheet

Case Manager: Jennifer Jones	**Student's Name:** Samantha Smith

This student has a disability and must receive specialized instruction, accommodations, modifications, and related services in accordance with his/her Individualized Educational Program. All teachers providing instruction and services for students with disabilities must be aware of the student's needs. The following information is confidential and must be kept in a secure location.

Student(s) Strengths, Interests, and Preferences:
- Above-average intelligence
- Strong verbal skills
- Strong social and interpersonal skills
- In-depth knowledge of animals, especially horses
- Participates in the 4H program and Girl Scouts
- Potential interest in becoming a veterinarian

Student(s) Challenges:
- Difficulty decoding text
- Difficulty following oral directions
- Easily frustrated when presented with reading assignments, will engage in avoidance activities
- Independent assignments frequently incomplete—may be due in part to a lack of support at home

Additional Relevant Information:
- Father has been unemployed for an extended period of time and mother has been recently diagnosed with cancer
- Grandmother lives at home and is primary contact for school-related matters
- Two younger siblings she frequently is responsible for supervising

Please see me if you have any other questions/concerns about this student. I will be her case manager for this year. I look forward to working with you to make sure this year is a positive experience for all of us. My contact information is:

Phone Number: 909-998-3355 ext. 111   **E-Mail:** jj@astschools.org

---

proactive by determining which students need which services is one step toward reaching a compromise. A blank worksheet for organizing this information is provided in the appendix.

To complete this worksheet, the first step is to review the students' IEPs in order to determine which students require what services. Place a check mark in the column titled required for the services to be provided to each student. Once you know the services required, work with the related services provider to determine the days and times those services will occur.

Notice that going horizontally on the worksheet there are multiple lines for each student. This is necessary because sometimes the services will occur on different days at different times. Once the days and times for the services are established, the teaching team in the self-contained setting can develop its daily classroom schedule. Table 3.2 is a completed example of this worksheet.

The last critical part of student-related planning that applies to all teachers in collaboratively taught classrooms relates to accommodations and modifications. The terms accommodations and modifications are often used interchangeably. However, they do not mean the same thing. A modification fundamentally alters the content of what is being taught or tested, an accommodation does not. Think of an accommodation as a mechanism for "leveling the playing field" so that a student with a disability can accurately demonstrate his or her knowledge and skill.

For example, a student may have a cognitive processing speed that makes it difficult for him to retrieve answers to items on tests. It is not that he does not know the answer. Instead he needs more time to process the question and then locate the answer in his memory. In this case, the accommodation of extended time allows the student to demonstrate his level of mastery of the subject matter.

Table 3.2. Service Providers

Student's Initials	Case Manager	Case Management and Related Services Providers										
		Speech			Occupational Therapy			Physical Therapy			Counseling		
		Required	Day(s)	Time	Required	Day(s)	Time	Required	Day(s)	Time	Required	Day(s)	Time
CJ	Sharpe	X	Mon	9:30									
DC	Sharpe				X	Tues	9:30						
						Thurs	10:30						
AJ	Greene	X	Wed	2:30							X	Mon	12:30
MS	Greene							X	Fri	1:00			

This assumes of course that the assessment is not measuring a student's fluency rate. If this was a measure of the number of words read correctly or the number of math facts completed accurately in a specific time, then providing extended time would become a modification. It would fundamentally alter the intent of the assessment.

Accommodations and modifications are often difficult for general education teachers to accept. Sometimes this is because of the vague nature of the accommodation. For example, what exactly is meant by "preferential seating" or "extended time"? A lack of clarity can lead to confusion.

Other times it is the one-size-fits-all approach that IEP teams take to providing the accommodations. When every student with an IEP requires the same accommodation, it does not lead teachers to believe the process is individualized. How seriously should the accommodations be taken if the results of the process are generic?

Furthermore, most of the accommodations listed in an IEP are generally accepted as the practices used by good teachers. Is it really necessary to prescribe to teachers that they provide clearly defined limits or frequent praise? If so, the problem is much larger than can be addressed by the content of this book.

The most common reason for general education teachers' concerns about accommodations relates to the issue of fairness. Commonly the argument made by the general education teacher is that the practice of providing an accommodation to one student makes it unfair to the other students. If the accommodation is in fact providing the student with a disability an unnecessary advantage that argument is plausible.

However, if the accommodation is accomplishing its intended purpose of providing the student with a disability the equal opportunity to demonstrate or acquire knowledge it is not a legitimate concern. That student needs that accommodation much the same as a person with poor eyesight needs glasses.

Everyone will not be treated the same in a successfully run co-taught classroom. Rather the teachers will do the best they can to meet the diverse needs of their students so each of them can acquire and demonstrate mastery of the expected curriculum content. In fact, accommodations (not modifications) will be made for students regardless of whether they have an IEP or not.

To meet the obligations established in each student's IEP, the teaching team must identify the accommodations required. It is helpful to have a master list for organizing this information. Each accommodation identified in the student's IEP gets a check mark in the appropriate box for that student. Table 3.3 is an example completed list. A blank copy of the worksheet for organizing this information is located in the appendix.

CLASSROOM NEEDS

The importance of commonly held classroom rules, routines, and academic expectations to differentiated instruction is analogous to the relationship between the wheels and the car they are on. Without the wheels, the car will not travel. Without commonly held expectations, differentiated instruction in a collaboratively taught classroom will not work.

In a collaboratively taught differentiated classroom students will frequently engage in multiple activities and will be placed in multiple group configurations. If a teacher has not firmly established classroom rules, routines, and academic expectations, differentiated instruction can lead to classroom chaos. The resulting loss of instructional time will likely have a negative impact on the academic achievement of students.

A collaboratively taught classroom adds another dimension to classroom management. Teachers frequently value different behaviors and have different classroom expectations. Furthermore, the temperament and personalities of different teachers often lead to different ways of responding to student misbehavior.

If the teachers assigned to a collaborative classroom do not take the time to establish common expectations prior to engaging in their work with students, two negative outcomes frequently result. First, the teachers provide students with conflicting directives. The resulting student confusion makes it difficult to have a classroom environment conducive to the learning process. Furthermore, if these children go home and share this state of affairs with their parents then these parents are likely view the situation with a high degree of concern.

Table 3.3. Accommodations at a Glance

Student Initials	Extra Time on Tests	Extra Time on Assignments	Textbooks on Tape	Reduce Number of Problems	Test in Small Group	Present Material Orally and in Writing	Oral and Written Directions	Fewer Items per page	Enlarge Page	Provide Study Guides	Do not penalize for spelling errors	Other
CJ	X	X		X								
DC			X			X	X		X			
AJ					X					X		
QP	X				X					X	X	
DF	X	X						X				X

Second, students figure out that one teacher is more likely than the other to provide the desired response. For example they ask teacher A to go to the bathroom because they know that teacher B is likely to say no to their request. When this happens repeatedly it leads to divisiveness and resentment between the teachers.

ESTABLISHING CLASSROOM RULES

Rules identify the general expectations for the classroom. Effectively establishing and maintaining these classroom rules makes it possible for the teachers to focus on increasing student achievement. Furthermore, these rules provide students with the structure they need in order to maintain engagement with instructional tasks. However, in order to be effective classroom rules must meet certain guidelines.

Before describing the guidelines for writing classroom rules, it is vital to first describe general guidelines for selecting the content of those rules. The content of any classroom rules must never conflict with the overall school or district rules. In order to maintain safety, order, and consistency school rules must be in effect in all classrooms at all times.

Within the classroom, the content of a rule should be applicable at all times. These rules must be consistent across situations and should not vary or change depending upon contexts or circumstances.

The number of classroom rules must be manageable. In general three to five well-written classroom rules is sufficient for a classroom. In order for a rule to be considered well written, it must meet four criteria.

First, the rule must be understandable. In other words, each classroom rule must be stated in a manner easily comprehended by students. This requires use of vocabulary that is consistent with the students' ages and abilities. If in doubt, make the wording simple.

Second, the rule must be doable. A classroom rule is of little value if the students are not capable of following it. To be effective, classroom rules must be within the students' maturation level and mental and physical abilities.

Third, the rule should be stated positively. More specifically, when wording a rule it is better to state what you want students to do than what you do not want them to do. Stating a rule positively encourages the desired behavior.

Fourth, the rule must be stated in behavioral terms. Rules are more easily understood and monitored when they are defined by action statements which begin with a verb. For example, the statement "Bring your notebook and a pen to every class" describes what students are expected to do.

Lastly, classroom rules should be posted and reviewed on a regular basis. Having the rules visible and reviewing them frequently reinforces their importance. Of course, classroom rules are typically an extension of a teacher's belief about how students learn best. This can create a dilemma when you have two teachers making this decision.

Activity 3.1 is a suggested activity for identifying and documenting the rules that will exist in a collaboratively taught classroom. If two teachers are spending the majority of the school day teaching in a collaborative classroom, it makes sense for them to complete this activity together.

However, if one of the collaborative teachers is split among multiple assignments, it would make more sense for this activity to be done collectively with all of the teachers involved. In this situation there may be some rules that are specific to a given type of class (e.g., a science lab) but other rules may be able to be mutually agreed upon for all of the involved classrooms.

ESTABLISHING ROUTINES

Routines are specific procedures to be used to carry out common classroom tasks. Routines include how students pass in their papers or sharpen their pencils. Much like rules, different teachers value different routines. In addition, even the same routine may be done differently in various teachers' classrooms.

Teaching students how to perform routines prevents behavioral problems and increases instructional time. When students know the expectations, they are less likely to engage in inappropriate behavior. Furthermore, even though it will take time to teach these routines in the beginning of the school year, once learned and established these routines will result in more time spent on academics over the remainder of the year.

> **Activity 3.1—Establishing Common Classroom Rules**
>
> **Time required:** 30–45 minutes
> **Materials:** Each partner will require a pen or pencil and paper
> **Steps:**
>
> 1. Separately each teacher should brainstorm a list of between three and seven potential classroom rules. These rules must meet the content guidelines stated above.
> 2. Still working separately, teachers will rank their potential classroom rules, with the number one being the most important.
> 3. Teachers will share their ranked list with their partner(s). In addition to stating the potential rule, he or she shall state the rationale for the importance of the rule. Partner(s) may only seek clarification for understanding at this point in the process.
> 4. Once each partner has stated their rank-ordered list of potential classroom rules and the supporting rationale, the partners shall engage in a discussion. This discussion should result in the partners developing one list that they understand and can agree to support.
> 5. Once the list has been agreed upon, the partners will use the previously stated criteria to finalize their classroom rules.

The routines that members of a collaborative teaching team select to teach and reinforce will vary based upon the age and abilities of their students. Below is a list of potential routines each collaborative teaching team should consider. This list may not encompass all potential routines, and some of them certainly are more appropriate for specific settings, thus partners should feel free to add to and delete from this list:

- Greeting and escorting students to and from school
- Signaling for student attention
- Requesting teacher assistance
- Asking questions
- Beginning the school day or class period
- Sharpening pencils
- Ending the school day or class period

- Turning in assignments
- Making up missed assignments
- Forming learning groups
- Going to the restroom, water fountain, nurse, or locker
- Lining up and walking in the halls
- Distributing and collecting materials and supplies

There must be a process for teaching students how to correctly complete each of these routines. The following procedure can be used to effectively teach any classroom procedure.

First, the teachers must tell the students the name of the routine to be learned. Providing a *brief* rationale emphasizing the importance of the skill is also important. Next, the students must be shown how the routine should be performed. This is best done by presenting one step at a time, with a visual demonstration accompanying each step. After that, students should perform the skill while the teachers provide feedback on their performance. From this point forward students will continue to practice the use of the skill. The teachers will monitor, reinforce, and when necessary re-teach the use of the routine.

Activity 3.2 should be used by the members of a collaborative teaching team in order to identify the routines required in their classroom. Once again, if two teachers are spending the majority of the school day teaching in a collaborative classroom, it makes sense for them to complete this activity together. However, if one of the collaborative teachers is split among multiple assignments, it would make more sense for this activity to be done collectively with all of the teachers involved.

An example of a worksheet completed during this activity can be seen in table 3.4. Note that this completed worksheet only represents the first page. Each identified routine requires completion of a separate "steps in the routine" box shown in table 3.5.

ESTABLISHING ACADEMIC EXPECTATIONS

Establishing common rules and routines is vitally important to the success of any collaborative teaching arrangement. Also vitally important

---

Activity 3.2—Identifying Routines

Time required: 30–45 minutes
Materials: Each partner will require a pen or pencil and a blank copy of table 3.4.
Steps:

1. Working as a team, review the list of common classroom routines identified in table 3.4. Place a check mark in the box to identify those routines you believe are necessary for the classroom you will be collaboratively teaching. In the spaces provided add any routines that you think need to be established that are not on this list.
2. For each identified routine identify and sequence the steps students will be expected to take in order to successfully complete the routine.
3. Prioritize your list of routines in order to determine the order and general time frame in which they will be taught.

---

is the development and communication of a common set of academic expectations. In particular, teachers and students must clearly understand how learning will be assessed and evaluated.

Due to the absence of clear school or district policies, determining final grades, providing extra credit assignments, allowing make-up work

Table 3.4. Potential Classroom Routines

☐ Greeting and escorting students to and from school	[X] Signaling for student attention
[X] Requesting teacher assistance	☐ Asking questions
[X] Beginning the school day or class period	☐ Sharpening pencils
[X] Ending the school day or class period	[X] Turning in assignments
[X] Making up missed assignments	☐ Forming learning groups
[X] Going to the restroom, water fountain, nurse, or locker	☐ Lining up and walking in the halls
☐ Distributing and collecting materials and supplies	Other:
Other:	Other:

Table 3.5. Steps in Routine (to be completed for each identified routine in Table 3.4)

Name of Routine: Turning in Assignments

1. Teacher provides signal—students stop what they are doing and look at teacher quietly.
2. Students check to make sure paper has the proper heading.
3. Students quietly wait for the papers in their row to be passed forward. Students place their paper on top of the papers they receive.
4. Once all of the papers reach the front desks, they are passed to the right.
5. Students wait quietly for the next set of instructions.

due to absence, and assessing penalties for turning in late assignments frequently vary from teacher to teacher. In many cases, teachers view these domains as decisions to be made via the use of their professional judgment. Thus, when two teachers with different backgrounds and experiences enter into a collaborative teaching arrangement they may have very different perspectives on academic expectations.

Obviously two teachers can't have different academic expectations for the students in a collaboratively taught classroom. In order to make sure there are consistent and clear academic expectations teachers should develop a course "syllabus" prior to teaching together. The contents and format of this "syllabus" will vary depending upon the age, ability, and maturity level of the students. However, at a minimum every syllabus should include:

- An explanation of how final grades will be determined;
- Procedures for making up missed assignments due to absence;
- Penalties (if any) for turning in late assignments;
- If provided, procedures for earning extra credit.

Other potentially valuable topics include:

- List of major learning goals for the year;
- Course description/outline;
- Penalties for academic dishonesty;
- Opportunities for extra help.

A sample syllabus can be seen in example 3.3.

Example 3.3 Sample Syllabus

XYZ SCHOOL
Course Syllabus

SUBJECT: Language Arts
TEACHERS: Mrs. Smith and Mr. Jones
GRADE: 8
COURSE DESCRIPTION: The language arts are integrative, interactive ways of communicating that develop through reading, writing, speaking, and listening. They are the means through which one is able to receive information; think logically and creatively; express ideas; and understand and participate meaningfully in spoken, written, and nonverbal communications. New literacy includes the ability to read, write, speak, and view in a variety of online environments that often involve communicating and collaborating across the globe. Students successfully completing the requirements for this class will demonstrate the ability to
(1) read a variety of texts with fluency and accurate comprehension;
(2) produce writing and speech that effectively communicates the intended message;
(3) listen accurately to information from various sources;
(4) Create, analyze, and critique information presented through visual images.

GRADING: The primary purpose for grading in this classroom is the communication of student progress toward the district's stated curriculum objectives. Final grades will be determined based on the average scores of weekly quizzes, unit tests, unit projects, and homework assignments. The value of each shall be:

- Unit tests—40%
- Weekly quizzes—20%
- Unit projects—30%
- Homework assignments—10%

LATE ASSIGNMENTS: Late work will be accepted, however the student shall lose 2% of the possible points that can be earned for that assignment for each day it is overdue. The maximum point loss will be 10%. Work that is not submitted will be identified as I (incomplete). Students are required to complete all assigned work and will be given opportunities to do so. This may include detention, supervised lunch, and other opportunities as appropriate and necessary.

(continued)

> **Example 3.3** *(Continued)*
>
> **ABSENCES:** Upon returning to school after an absence for any reason, a student has the number of days equal to the length of that absence to submit any missed assignments without penalty. After that time period the policy on late assignments cited above will apply.
>
> **EXTRA CREDIT:** Extra credit opportunities may be made available throughout the course of the school year. Any points earned for the successful completion of extra credit assignments will be added to the student's final average. A student with incomplete assignments will not be eligible to complete extra credit assignments.

ESTABLISHING RESPONSIBILITIES

As a profession, teaching involves much more than managing student behavior, assessing learning, and providing instruction. There are many responsibilities teachers must assume in order to make sure a classroom and school function effectively. In a classroom taught by a single teacher it is easy to decide who is responsible for completing each assigned task.

In a collaboratively taught classroom there is the possibility for increased efficiency through a divided workload. However, this does not happen without conscious consideration of who will be responsible for completing the various classroom tasks. With clarity regarding responsibilities it is far more likely that all of the required tasks will be accomplished. Without this clarity, tasks can fall through the cracks, creating unnecessary tension among partners.

Table 3.6 is a chart listing common classroom responsibilities. These responsibilities are divided into those that happen daily, those that happen regularly and do not require a great deal of discussion, and those which are ongoing that should be discussed thoroughly.

There is one column for the special services provider and a second column for the general education teacher. Ideally the co-teaching partners should decide who will be responsible for each task prior to working with their students. A check mark or explanation could be placed in the box under the column of the responsible teacher.

Table 3.6. Chart of Responsibilities

Responsibility	Special Services Provider	General Education Teacher
Daily Responsibilities		
Making photocopies		
Taking attendance		
Collecting work		
Passing out assignments		
Walking with students to specials or lunch		
Picking up students from specials or lunch		
Ongoing Responsibilities—Minimal Discussion Required		
Creating and maintaining substitute teacher plans		
Modifying instructional materials and assessments		
Reserving instructional spaces		
Changing bulletin boards and displays		
Updating classroom website		
Scheduling meetings		
Ongoing Responsibilities—Decisions Required		
Same person for all students or divided? If so, how?		
• Completing interim reports		
• Returning parent phone calls or e-mails		
• Initiating parent contact		
• Assigning/submitting final grades		
• Creating tests and assessments		
• Maintaining student records		
Completing required reports: • Who will complete which reports?		
Maintaining grade book: • One grade book with all students or separate?		

These responsibilities will likely change and evolve over time. However, it is vital to the long-term success of the teachers that they get off to a good start. The structure of knowing who is responsible for completing tasks is reassuring and can create positive momentum.

CLASSROOM SPACE

Imagine that you are going to be spending an extensive amount of time living in another person's home. When you are present in this person's home you feel uncomfortable because you do not like the décor and the space does not meet your functional needs. However, because you are a guest you do not feel right expressing your opinions. You simply live with your feelings, never quite getting comfortable in that space.

This is the same type of experience many special education teachers have when they are assigned to work with a general education teacher in that teacher's classroom. For this reason, if the special education teacher is going to be assigned to work in a general education classroom for the majority of the day then both should be assigned to a new room. This level of disruption would not make sense if the special education teacher was only going to be in the classroom for short periods of time.

The general education teacher may not like this move, especially if he or she has been in the classroom for many years. Yet for the teachers there is no better "getting to know you" activity than the shared experience of arranging and decorating a new classroom. Regardless of whether the classroom location is new, there are some guidelines to consider when arranging a collaboratively taught classroom.

First, the use of physical space sends a clear message about the relationship between the teachers. If the room is going to be shared for a large portion of the school day, then both teachers should have a desk in that room.

Furthermore, anything used to identify that classroom should include both teachers' names. This includes the nameplate outside the door, letters to parents identifying their child's teachers, and report cards. If the room is only shared for shorter periods, then the special services provider should be given a space in that room to place personal items and professional materials.

If assigned seating is to be used then students identified as requiring support services should be evenly distributed throughout the classroom. At times it may be necessary to pull these students together for instruction, but seating all of these students in close proximity to one another sends a strong negative message about the status of these students in the classroom. Seating the students that require support services in clusters creates "islands in the mainstream." The students may be sharing the same physical space, but they are not really members of the class.

After reviewing the identified needs of the students it may be necessary to make changes to how the classroom is arranged. For example, if the class will include a student that is wheelchair bound then it is important to plan the space so that every area of the classroom is accessible.

If the class will include a student that is easily distracted then all unnecessary distractions should be eliminated. If the class will include a student that has demonstrated impulsive, destructive behaviors then all of the potential tools that could be used to harm one's self or others should be placed in secure places.

Lastly, the strategies used in a collaboratively taught differentiated classroom will require a place for small group instruction. Some classrooms will be so crowded that it may not be possible to include a designated space for this type of activity. If this is the case, it is necessary to identify the other spaces that are available for use during the time when co-teaching is occurring.

To be effective a collaborative teaching team must take the time prior to the start of a school year to perform certain tasks. Determining the classroom rules, routines, academic expectations, and use of physical space will provide the foundation upon which differentiated instruction can occur. Without these things confusion, division, and ultimately ineffectiveness are likely to result. Yet these things by themselves are insufficient. To differentiate instruction effectively, collaborative teachers must have the ability to accurately assess students' current levels of knowledge and skill. This is the subject of chapter four.

Points to Remember

- Accommodations are fair when they provide a student with an equal opportunity to acquire or demonstrate knowledge and skills.

- Prior to working with students, co-teachers should establish mutually agreed upon classroom rules and routines, responsibilities, and academic expectations.
- In addition to being important for practical reasons like accessibility and safety, the use of classroom space sends a powerful message to teachers and students.

CHAPTER 4

Assessment for and of Learning

The topic of assessment is difficult to place in the sequence of the instructional cycle. Assessment is used prior to instruction for diagnosing students' current levels of knowledge and skill. In addition, it is used during instruction for monitoring students' levels of understanding. Having this information during the instructional phase enables the teacher to make any necessary adjustments. Lastly, it is used at the conclusion of instruction to make inferences about and then communicate students' performance levels. Thus, while this chapter precedes the one on instructional planning, it could easily have been placed after the chapter on instruction.

This chapter begins with an explanation of several key assessment concepts. Next, it provides suggestions for developing and scoring effective assessment tools. Lastly, the chapter concludes with the provision of guidelines for determining grades in a collaboratively taught classroom.

ASSESSMENT BASICS

Often educators give an assessment to their students and then confidently draw conclusions about students' knowledge and skills. This is done even though no single assessment is capable of producing the quality of information necessary for making an accurate judgment of a student's knowledge and skill.

Classroom assessments can take many different forms. For example, classroom assessment can be paper and pencil, observation, oral, or performance-based, to name just a few. Each of the forms of assessment is better suited for assessing different aspects of student learning.

Combining data from various assessment tools to measure students' knowledge and skills will result in a "union of insufficiencies." In turn this union will provide a picture of student learning closer to his or her true abilities.

At best, assessment is an inference-making enterprise in which we formally collect overt evidence from students to make what we hope are accurate inferences about a student's status with respect to covert, educationally important variables. The accuracy of these inferences is critical because the teacher's understanding of a student's knowledge and skills should form the basis for a teacher's instructional decisions.

If assessment data is to serve as a guide to instructional planning and be used for providing feedback to students then the data must come from high-quality tools. One critical defining feature of a high-quality assessment tool is content validity.

Content validity is the property of an assessment in which the sample of items reflects the universe of items from which the assessment is designed. In other words, does the collection of items required to complete the assessment fairly represent all of the items that could have been selected? Is the number of items on the assessment reflective of the amount of time spent on teaching each topic? If the answer to these two questions is yes, then the content validity of the assessment is high.

A second critical defining feature of high-quality assessment tools is reliability. When an assessment is reliable the results obtained will be consistent. For the purpose of classroom assessment, there are two main types of reliability.

Inter-rater reliability is the degree of agreement two different raters would demonstrate if they were assessing the same performance. If two different raters both rate a performance similarly then there is a high degree of inter-rater reliability.

Intra-rater reliability is the degree to which the same rater would give the same rating if the performance was rated again at another time. If a rater scores the performance similarly regardless of when that scoring occurs then there is a high degree of intra-rater reliability.

To obtain the most accurate assessment data, teachers must strive to improve the reliability and validity of their assessments. The following list contains guidelines teachers can use to achieve this goal:

- Write clear student directions;
- Use standardized administration procedures;
- Increase the number of sample items;
- Increase the frequency of assessments;
- Unless it is a fluency assessment, provide ample time for students to complete the task;
- Avoid poorly worded, ambiguous, or tricky assessment prompts;
- Develop your assessments in advance of instruction;
- Only rate the aspects of the performance being assessed. If it is a spelling test then count spelling errors. If you are assessing content knowledge then limit your rating to the demonstration of content knowledge. Students can still be required to correct mistakes without it having to become a part of the performance rating.
- Use high-quality rubrics or scoring guides to increase the objectivity of scoring;
- Minimize the impact of student factors. For example, if possible avoid administering an assessment to a student demonstrating a high level of fatigue or a strong emotional state.
- Minimize the impact of teacher factors. For example, if possible avoid attempting to assess a response when rushed or hungry.
- Minimize the impact of environmental factors. For example, do not administer or score an assessment in a location characterized by uncomfortable temperatures or frequent distractions.

Regardless of how well co-teachers follow these guidelines, they must bear in mind the fact that the data obtained likely does not represent everything a student knows about the topic. We can and we should reduce assessment errors by increasing the validity and reliability of the assessments. However, despite our best efforts, no single assessment tool will yield perfect results.

PAPER AND PENCIL TESTS

Paper and pencil tests traditionally consist of a mixture of forced-choice, essay, and short answer items. For each of these item types, there are specific actions that should be taken to improve the probability students will provide a response demonstrating their current level of knowledge or skill.

Short answer and completion items are frequently used to assess lower-level thinking skills such as memorization or basic knowledge. These items have both advantages and disadvantages.

First, because an answer must be recalled and not simply recognized, the possibility of guessing the correct answer is minimized. Second, because they are flexible and relatively easy to write, many of these items can be used on a single assessment. Yet the scoring of short answer items is often subjective and items in which a single answer to the question is correct are difficult to create.

If you have the choice it is better to create a short answer question than one that requires the completion of a statement. Questions are clearer and more straightforward, thus leaving less room for ambiguity. For example, instead of providing the stem, "Separatists wanted to avoid _____," ask "What did the Separatists want to avoid?"

Avoid providing grammatical clues that will narrow down the potentially correct answers. The use of the word "an" in the question "An _____ hunts at night and sounds like it cries, 'Hoo, hoo'" provides the clue that the answer must start with a vowel or the letter h.

The blanks in completion items should be placed near the end of the stem. When the blank appears near the beginning of the stem, students are more likely to get stuck, not being able to move past this initial part. When the blank comes near the end of the stem, the student has been prepared by the preceding information.

Consider the following question: "'To' is a preposition, whereas _____ and _____ are other parts of speech." It is completely possible to know the correct answer to this question and yet not be able to provide it. The information in the stem is not sufficient to make clear what the question is asking for. Better would be "'To' is a preposition, whereas other parts of speech that sound the same are _____ and two."

Lastly, short answer and completion items should be written so that there is only one correct answer. The question "The United States Secret Service was created in 1862 in order to _____" has too many potentially correct answers.

Due to processing difficulties some students will not be able to retrieve stored knowledge. This does not mean they can't recognize the correct answer if it is presented to them. A word bank changes fill-in-the-blank items from a recall task to one that requires recognition.

When using word banks it is important to include more plausible words and phrases to complete the blanks than the number of blanks available. This increases the probability that the correct answer will not be achieved through the process of elimination.

Another possibility is the provision of partial letter clues for the missing words. These partial clues do not give the student the answer. Instead they provide the student with retrieval cues they can use to access the information if it has been stored in memory. If the student does not know the answer "Continental Army," the clues provided in the question "George Washington was the leader of the C_____ A_____" will not help the test-taker provide the correct answer.

Essay questions are an excellent choice when the goal is accessing higher-order thinking and reasoning skills. Like short answer and completion items, essay questions are relatively easy to write. In addition, because the response is extended, the risk of cheating is reduced.

On the other hand, the extended nature of the responses limits the scope of sampling. Furthermore, answers to essay questions can be difficult to score. Lastly, the emphasis on producing written language can make it difficult for some students to demonstrate their knowledge.

High-quality essay questions are complete and clear. More specifically, the question is precise regarding what is required in a successful answer. Consider the difference between "Discuss the impact of the Civil War on the economy of the postwar South" and "Discuss the impact of the Civil War on the economy of the postwar South, taking into account the following factors: reduction in the work force, international considerations, and the changing role of agriculture." The second question is much clearer regarding the content the test takers should include in their answers.

Scoring the answers to essay questions can be difficult. Assessor fatigue is a major threat to intra-rater reliability. If at all possible essay questions should be scored in batches, with rest breaks taken as necessary. Having a model correct answer to use as a basis for comparison or a rubric can improve inter-rater reliability. This is especially important when co-teachers decide to divide the task of assessing. A student's response should not receive different ratings based on whose pile it was placed in.

Obviously essay questions put students with writing disabilities at a disadvantage. It is important for teachers of these students to decide if an essay is required to demonstrate the learning. There is only one way to demonstrate the ability to write a five-paragraph essay. There are many ways to demonstrate knowledge of scientific concepts, historical events, and similar types of content.

Multiple choice questions continue to be very common on classroom assessments. To some degree this is due to the fact that they are easy to score. In addition, their effectiveness is relatively easy to analyze. On the other hand, for a number of reasons these types of questions are difficult to write correctly.

A common practice is to include answer choices like "all of the above" or combinations like "A and B" in the set of possible answers. This practice stems from an effort by test developers to trick students into selecting the wrong answer. For a question to be included in a standardized assessment only 40 percent to 60 percent of the students must select the correct answer. Having "all of the above" or combination answers will result in some students who know the correct answer selecting the wrong one.

The practice of using distracters to get questions to "behave properly" is valuable to test developers seeking to create norm-referenced tests. It is not valuable for assessment situations in which we seek to determine if a student has learned the content. Never use "all of the above" as an answer choice for a multiple choice question. However, the use of "none of the above" does have merit for making items more demanding.

Much like fill-in-the-blank questions, teachers must be careful to avoid providing grammar clues indicating the correct answer. It is also important to make the stem of the item self-contained, clear, and precise. Consider the question stem "New York City is the site of the next Olympics and _____." The fact that the question stem is incomplete makes comprehension of the question far more difficult. A better example of a clear, precise, complete stem is "The current population of New York City is _____."

Double negatives in a stem create confusion. Consider the following stem: "Not only do cicadas come every 17 years, but they never arrive _____." It is completely possible to know the answer being sought but be so confused by the stem that a wrong answer is given.

All of the answer choices provided should be plausible. If not, then the process of elimination can be used to increase the chances of guessing a correct answer. Lastly, the questions need to be independent of one another. In other words, the answer on one question should not give the test taker the answer to another question.

Students with visual perceptual problems can have difficulty reading the answers to multiple choice questions that are listed vertically. This is especially true when the answer choices are identified by letters. Students with this type of disability benefit from having answers that are listed horizontally and are preceded with bullets or numbers. Furthermore, allowing these students to circle the correct answer instead of writing it on a line will help to avoid the problem of placing correct answers in the wrong answer spaces.

Despite the fact that matching questions usually emphasize memorization and assess lower levels of knowledge, they remain common. Perhaps this is because they are straightforward, are easy to administer and score, and decrease the probability of guessing a correct answer.

Commonly the first column contains the premises. The second column contains the matching options. A well-designed set of matching items will contain more options than premises. Once again, this reduces the risk of selecting the correct answer based solely upon the process of elimination.

The longer part of the match should be in the premise column. Students must keep their understanding of the premise in working memory while they scan the options column to select the correct match. Matching items are not intended to assess the effectiveness of a student's working memory.

Placing the premises in an order that makes sense also assists with comprehension. For example, if possible organize the premises in an alphabetical or chronological sequence. Also, if it makes sense to do so, label each column. These two practices will orient and thus assist the test takers.

Lastly, make sure that all of the premises and responses appear on the same page. This may mean that the number of items in the set will need to be reduced. The practice of presenting sets of questions and answers in smaller groups is an especially effective strategy when assessing students with written language disabilities.

True or false test items are valuable when there is a clear, unequivocal distinction between two alternatives. This type of question is difficult to write unless the most basic facts are being assessed. Thus, successfully answering this type of question requires the memorization of discrete bits of knowledge. While they are easy to score and many of them can be administered in a short amount of time, the probability of guessing correctly on true or false items makes them a poor choice for assessment of learning.

With that said, if a teacher intends to use true or false items, there are several general guidelines to follow. First, true or false items must always be stated as a declarative sentence. Second, a quality true or false question focuses on only one idea, concept, or topic. Lastly, beware of using qualifiers such as "always," "never," "sometimes," and so on. Savvy test takers will realize that few things are always or never true, so they will successfully select false as the answer. Thus, the student gets the correct answer by using a test-taking strategy rather than knowledge.

PERFORMANCE TASKS AND RUBRICS

An effective means for assessing students' ability to apply knowledge and skills is to have them complete a performance task. Performance tasks require students to construct their responses and apply their knowledge. Some performance tasks are authentic because they mirror "real life" situations while others are more contrived. Similarly, some performance tasks are highly structured to fit a specific instructional objective whereas others require demonstration of the application of numerous instructional objectives.

When constructing a performance task, there are several guidelines to follow. First, students should be given some degree of choice in task selection. Second, the successful completion of the task should require both the elaboration of essential content knowledge and the use of specific processes. Third, the product should be assessed via an explicit scoring system.

Example 4.1 is an example performance task designed to assess the oral presentation skills of fifth-grade students.

An explicit scoring system can be developed by creating an analytical rubric in advance of students' task completion. An example of this type of rubric can be seen in table 4.1. These types of rubrics have the potential to pinpoint students' specific gaps and deficiencies.

Through their use, teachers can identify and then target areas of weakness that then serve as the focus for the differentiation of instruction. Furthermore, they help students identify and potentially internalize the qualitative differences associated with excellent work. Guidelines for successfully writing an analytical rubric include the following:

- Have multiple scoring levels in which a zero represents no evidence or effort and the highest score represents what students must do to exceed the standard.

Example 4.1 Performance Task Assessment

ANYTOWN USA
SPEAKING ASSESSMENT

STUDENT NAME: _____

TEACHER: _____

GRADE: 5   PROMPT # 1

DIRECTIONS: You will have 30 minutes to prepare for the speaking task that follows. You may practice, write notes on cards, or do anything else you think will assist you in making this oral presentation during this 10-minute time period. You will not be assessed on your preparation, only your presentation. Your presentation is limited to a maximum of 3 minutes. As you make your presentation, keep in mind your audience and purpose.

TASK DESCRIPTION: Tell about a time when you were really surprised. Include what it was that surprised you, why you were surprised, and anything else you think would be interesting or important to share.

- Identify the domains of knowledge and skills that are critical to successful completion of the task.
- Within each domain and level write concise specific descriptors of what the knowledge or skill would look like at that level of achievement. Use of vocabulary from the curriculum goals is often helpful to achieve this outcome. In the example rubric, the category of adequate command represents meeting the objectives identified in the district's curriculum guides.
- Provide a space to tally each domain score. While not essential, these scores can be totaled to produce an overall score.
- To increase the accuracy of scoring, place a score between columns if the student demonstrates some, but not all, of the behavior expected at a given level. For example, a student demonstrates some of the nonverbal behaviors required to earn a 3, but not all of them. As long as they meet all of the criteria for the score of 1, it is perfectly acceptable to give that student a score of 2 even though that is not an option on this rubric.

Performance tasks and analytical rubrics are challenging to write and often take substantial time to develop. In addition, the tasks also require extended amounts of time for students to complete. Yet no other assessment provides better evidence of a student's ability to apply knowledge and skills to real or simulated problems. For this reason performance tasks scored via analytical rubrics should be a part of assessment practices in every classroom.

TEACHER OBSERVATION

Teacher observation is another method of assessing students' ability to complete tasks. Like performance tasks scored via analytical rubrics, observation can be a highly effective means of assessing performance of skills like oral reading or public speaking. However, observations can also be used to assess non-academic factors like behavior and effort.

Gathering data through teacher observation can be done through the completion of observation checklists or through structured interviews. Observation checklists are tools used to record the specific skills or

Table 4.1. Sample Rubric

Score	Limited Command 1	Adequate Command 3	Strong Command 5	Total Score
Organization	Audience cannot understand presentation because of poor organization: • Introduction is undeveloped or irrelevant. • Main points and conclusion are unclear	Satisfactory organization: • Clear introduction. • Main points are well stated. • Clear conclusion.	Superb organization: • Clear and engaging introduction. • Main points are well stated, with each point leading to next point. • Clear summary and conclusion.	
Oral Delivery	Oral delivery impedes understanding of the presentation: • Audience members have difficulty hearing the presentation. • Nonfluencies ("ums") are used excessively. • Articulation and pronunciation tend to be sloppy.	Satisfactory oral delivery: • Generally, articulation and pronunciation are clear. • Some use of nonfluencies is observed. • Audience members can hear the presentation.	Superb oral delivery: • Natural, confident delivery that does not just convey the message, but enhances it. • Excellent use of voice volume and pace.	

(continued)

Table 4.1. (Continued)

	Limited Command 1	Adequate Command 3	Strong Command 5	Total Score
Score				
Nonverbal Behaviors	Nonverbal behaviors distract from the message of the presentation: • Limited eye contact. • Movements are jerky or excessive. • Distracting gestures evident.	Satisfactory nonverbal behaviors: • Effective use of eye contact. • Minimal to no distracting gestures. • Posture is appropriate.	Superb nonverbal behaviors: • Posture, eye contact, smooth gestures, and facial expressions indicate confidence and a willingness to communicate.	
Audience Awareness	Appears unaware of audience. • Seems unaware of audience reactions. • Provides brief or irrelevant responses to audience questions.	Satisfactory audience awareness: • Aware of audience reactions. • Answers audience questions adequately.	Superb audience awareness: • Modifies delivery of presentation based on audience reactions. • Goes beyond simply answering audience questions by providing explanations or elaborations that interest the audience members.	

behaviors of students. As record-keeping devices, checklists can track who has mastered a target skill.

The first step in creating an observation checklist is the development of specific behavioral indicators that represent mastery of the targeted performance skill. It is difficult for two independent raters to agree upon the demonstration of a broadly defined behavior like persistence. Much more reliable is the observation and recording of concrete behaviors. For example, persistence can be observed through specific behaviors, such as when the initial attempt is unsuccessful, the student tries several approaches or brainstorms alternative strategies.

It is difficult to observe and record during the act of instructing. Having a co-teacher makes it possible for the recording of data to occur while the other teacher is engaged in providing instruction to the students. This is especially valuable when attempting to develop appropriate behavioral interventions.

Development of appropriate behavioral intervention plans is based upon data. More specifically, to understand and intervene effectively teachers must first identify what comes before the undesirable behavior occurs (the antecedent), what the behavior is, and what happens after the behavior is demonstrated (the consequence). It is also helpful to know the frequency and duration of the undesirable behavior.

Knowing the antecedent could lead to changes that prevent the behavior from occurring. Knowing the consequence of the undesirable behavior could lead to a change in reinforcement practices. If you know the frequency and duration of the undesirable behaviors, then there is a baseline for determining progress.

Interviews and conferences with students are yet another way to probe students' understandings of topics. These interactions often yield information that cannot be ascertained in any other way. In fact, it could be argued that this form of assessment is the most valid for teachers to use when attempting to determine students' knowledge of a given concept.

To be used effectively, the teachers should decide on the questions they will ask and the method they will use for rating responses prior to conducting the interviews or conferences. Once the questions and ratings have been decided upon, the teachers must dedicate a block of time to meet with students. It is important to the process that the remaining students are provided with an activity they can do independently during this time. Clear expectations for the behavior of the rest of the class as well as for what students must bring to the interview or conference will make the process move much more smoothly.

GRADES

Assigning grades to students with disabilities in co-taught classrooms can present a dilemma. It seems unfair and counterproductive to assign a poor grade to a student with a disability when that student has made a strong effort to complete assignments and participated in class on a regular basis. Yet assigning an inflated grade to a student who has not met the established performance expectations provides an inaccurate picture of that student's achievement.

Compounding the dilemma are the fallacies that educators believe or have been told regarding grading practices. Contrary to popular belief, a student with an individualized education plan may receive a failing grade in a course. Through the appropriate supports and services the individualized education plan must provide the student with a disability the opportunity to receive passing grades and advance in grade level with his or her peers. It is not a guarantee of a passing grade.

Another misconception is that report cards cannot identify a student's status as an exceptional learner. Because a report card is intended to communicate information about a student's achievement to the student, parents, and teachers, not third parties (like transcripts), a student's special status can appear on a report card. However, even on report cards schools must think carefully about when and why such information would be necessary.

Teachers rarely receive any guidance on how to assign grades to exceptional learners. The following guidelines are intended to serve as a decision-making model for assigning grades to students with disabilities in a collaboratively taught classroom.

If the student is able to meet the standard without any adaptations then no change in the grading process is required. If the standards are not appropriate for the student, then the teachers must determine what type of adaptations are required.

Accommodations do not change the content standards. Accommodations change the manner by which mastery of that content may be demonstrated. For example, the student requires extended time to complete an in-class test. Unless it is a measure of fluency, the student is still being required to demonstrate the same content knowledge. If the student is only receiving accommodations it is appropriate to use the standard method of determining grades.

Modifications result in changes to the standards. For example, suppose the standard required students to sort coins and make change. Looking at this standard, the student's IEP team decides this is too difficult for the student; they change it so the student will demonstrate the ability to identify pennies, nickels, dimes, and quarters. In this case the grade should be based on the student's progress toward the modified standard and not the grade-level standard.

When a grade is provided based on modified standards educators may decide to communicate this on the report card. In this case it is legal to include a notation such as an asterisk indicating that the grade reflects achievement on modified standards. This notation may also direct readers to the source for locating the modified standards.

Points to Remember

- Assessment is an inference-making process in which we attempt to ascertain what students know and can do.
- No single assessment is capable of providing sufficient data to accurately assess a student's level of understanding or performance.
- High levels of validity and reliability are the hallmarks of quality assessments.
- Different types of assessment are appropriate for assessing different types of knowledge and skills.
- High quality assessment is a prerequisite to effective differentiated instructional practices.

CHAPTER 5

Instructional Planning and Preparation

High-quality instructional planning is a prerequisite to effective collaborative teaching. When the teachers assigned to instruct collaboratively do not plan together in a substantial manner, a lack of parity is destined to occur. Without clear understanding of the learning objectives, teaching strategies, and assessment methods, the special services provider usually ends up in the role of floating and supporting students. This role could be easily filled for less money by a classroom aide.

The biggest barrier to collaborative planning is time. Regular common planning time is ideal and serves as a symbolic indicator of administrative support. However, making this model work successfully frequently requires more time than can be provided by the school district during the normal teacher work day. Often this is the case during the first year of two teachers working together regardless of how much common planning time they are given.

When common planning periods cannot be assigned, creative options must be considered. Each of the following options requires a degree of administrative support.

- Substitute coverage—two substitute teachers are assigned to rotate through the school day on a schedule that provides coverage for the collaborative teachers. During this covered class time, the teachers can meet to create instructional plans.
- Faculty meetings—if a meeting does not require their presence, collaborative teaching teams may be dismissed to create common instructional plans.

- School assemblies—if a particular assembly does not require the presence of all of the teachers then co-teaching teams may be dismissed to create plans.
- E-mail—teachers can work from separate locations to complete the appropriate sections of a joint lesson plan.
- Common Plan Book—teachers share one plan book. One of the teachers completes his or her section of the plan and then provides it via a staff mailbox for the other to review and finalize.

INSTRUCTIONAL PLANNING BASICS

Prior to moving sequentially through the planning process, it is important to address a few key concepts. The first of these key concepts is how to use the common planning time provided as effectively and efficiently as possible.

Structure improves the use of a team's planning time. More specifically, if possible the team should meet on a regular basis at the same time and in the same location. Typically, if a specific meeting time and date are not established, co-planning gets cast aside in favor of other pressing demands. In addition, having the same location for these meetings often results in all of the necessary materials being readily available.

Each meeting should consist of an agenda. This agenda does not have to be excessive, nor does it have to be formal. Instead, the teachers participating should determine at the onset of the meeting the items needing to be addressed and the approximate amount of time they expect each item will take. The act of listing these items and their approximate time frame encourages effective time management. A completed template teachers could use to structure their meetings is provided in table 5.1. A blank copy of this template can be found in the appendix.

The first item for each meeting must be instructional planning. As much as this seems like common sense, frequently a great deal of meeting time is lost dealing with non-instructional matters, student behaviors, and parental concerns. Student and parent issues, as well as other tasks, can be addressed when or if there is time remaining. Furthermore, this planning time must be protected. The message that this time is sacred must be communicated and reinforced when other demands are presented.

Table 5.1. Meeting Log Template

MEETING LOG		
Date: 12/1/2011	Start Time: 9:00	End Time: 9:30

AGENDA	
Items:	Time Limit
1. Planning next unit of instruction for math	20 minutes
2. Social studies project requirements	5 minutes
3. Mrs. Jones concerns—update on phone call	5 minutes
4.	
5.	

ACTION PLAN		
Action Items	Person Responsible	By When?
1. Modify social studies project	Mrs. Smith	12/4
2. Call Mrs. Jones	Mr. Adams	12/2
3.		

AGENDA FOR NEXT MEETING		
Date: 12/3	Time: 9:00	Location: Room 12

Expected Topics:
1. Report card grades
2. Grading persuasive essays
3.

It is distressing to see how often teachers re-create the wheel. During a year two teachers co-plan their instruction for an entire course or grade-level subject area. Then for whatever reason these teachers' assignments are switched. With this switch, frequently their lesson plans and materials enter the abyss. This is a waste of time and resources.

A school or district can create, either virtually or through hardcopies stored in a filing cabinet, a location to store all of the collaboratively developed lesson plans and differentiated instructional materials. Teachers entering new situations will then be able to use these materials as a starting point instead of starting from scratch.

ANNUAL PLANNING

Instructional planning begins with a clear understanding of the annual curricular goals to be learned by the students. These goals may come from state standards or local curriculum guides. Regardless of where they come from, it is vital that both teachers begin the planning process with a clear understanding of what students should know and be able to do by the end of the school year.

In order to obtain this clarity it is valuable to initially identify and sequence the units of instruction to be taught. A unit of study is a group of lessons lasting between two and eight weeks in which related instructional goals are taught. In math, the focus of the unit might be decimals. In science, the focus of the unit of instruction might be magnets and magnetism. Units of instruction may also focus on cross-disciplinary themes such as bravery or tolerance.

It is likely that the general education teacher who is more familiar with the content will provide the majority of input when completing this task. Table 5.2 is a completed example of an annual planning template for a fifth-grade language arts class. A blank copy of every form presented in this chapter can be found in the appendix.

IDENTIFYING INSTRUCTIONAL GOALS

With the units identified and sequenced, it is now possible to focus on developing each specific unit of instruction. Within each unit, there will be multiple instructional goals. Even within a single goal, there may be multiple things students must know and be able to do. Consider the following example: students will demonstrate the ability to read, write, and compare decimals to the thousandths. In fact, this is three separate goals listed in a single goal statement.

Table 5.2. Annual Instructional Guide

Subject Area: Language Arts **Teachers:** Mrs. Smith and Mrs. Jones	**Grade Level:** 5
Unit Title	*Anticipated Pacing*
Reading biographies	September
Reading and writing personal narratives	October
Reading and writing folk tales	November
Persuasive writing	December
Understanding advertisements/advertising strategies	January
Reading and comprehending everyday text	January
Public speaking	February
Research and inquiry skills	March–April
Reading and writing poetry	May–June

The most effective starting point for beginning the process of planning a unit of instruction is to examine the instructional goals you intend to include in the curriculum unit. More specifically, these goals must be broken down into those things each student must know and be able to do.

Suppose a fifth-grade language arts curriculum guide listed the standard **3.1:** *students will demonstrate the ability to speak in clear, concise, organized language that varies in content and form for different audiences and purposes*. Underneath that standard are the following objectives:

- **3.1.1** Students will demonstrate the ability to prepare and deliver a two-to-three-minute oral presentation that includes an introduction, main ideas, and a conclusion.
- **3.1.2** Students will demonstrate the ability to deliver a speech using the standard conventions of English, clear articulation, and appropriate voice volume and pace.
- **3.1.3** Students will demonstrate the ability to use nonverbal elements of delivery to maintain audience interest.
- **3.1.4** Students will demonstrate awareness of audience members' reactions to the content and delivery of their oral presentations.
- **3.1.5** Students will demonstrate the ability to ask audience members if they have questions and provide an adequate response to the questions asked.

Using this standard and these objectives, this fifth-grade unit of instruction on public speaking could be broken down into the example in table 5.3.

PRE-ASSESSMENT

Just like instructional planning is a prerequisite to effective co-teaching, high-quality data is a prerequisite to effective instructional planning. To obtain high-quality data for planning purposes requires the use of pre-instructional assessments.

Pre-instructional assessments are designed to gather information on students' current level of knowledge and skills in relation to the level they are expected to demonstrate at the end of the instructional cycle. Using the assessment principles and tools provided in the previous chapter, the teachers should generate a pre-assessment.

Table 5.3. Unit Worksheet

Unit of Instruction Planning Worksheet: Public Speaking		
Subject Area: Language Arts **Grade Level:** 5th **Teachers:** Mrs. Smith and Mrs. Jones		
Students Must Know	*Students Must Understand*	*Students Must Be Able to Do*
The parts of a formal speech: introduction, body, and conclusion.	The relationship between the audience's reactions during the speech and the speaker's need to make modifications during the delivery of the speech.	Identify an appropriate topic for a two-to-three-minute formal speech.
The basic qualities that define an effective introduction, body, and conclusion.	The relationship between the organization of the speech and the ability of the audience to comprehend the speaker's message.	Write a draft of formal speech topic that includes an introduction, body, and conclusion.
The basic qualities that define the effective oral delivery of a formal speech.	The relationship between the quality of the speaker's oral delivery and the audience members' ability to comprehend the speaker's message.	Use proper articulation, pronunciation, voice volume, and pace to effectively deliver a formal speech.
The basic nonverbal behaviors that enhance or detract from the delivery of a formal speech.	The relationship between the speaker's nonverbal behaviors and the audience members' level of engagement.	Use posture, eye contact, gestures, and facial expressions to effectively deliver a formal speech.
The basic qualities of an effective answer to an audience member's question.		Modify the delivery of their formal speech in reaction to the cues displayed by audience members.
The meaning of the terms: articulation, pronunciation, non-fluencies, voice volume, pace, gestures, and facial expressions.		Ask for and then adequately answer audience questions.

This pre-assessment will help the teachers determine the students' current knowledge or skill in the most critical focus areas for the unit of instruction. A thoughtful analysis of the results of the pre-assessment will make it possible for the teacher to identify the gaps in each student's learning and then plan instruction accordingly.

The remainder of this chapter will describe a process co-teachers can use to develop data-driven, differentiated instructional plans. Aspects of this process may look different depending upon the content being taught. However, using the basic concepts of this planning process will result in plans that will facilitate all students reaching higher levels of performance.

COMPLETING A UNIT PLAN

At this point teachers planning for co-instruction will know the skills and knowledge students must possess in order to meet the instructional goals established. Furthermore, if they have done the diagnostic pre-assessment described in the previous paragraphs then they will have an idea of their students' current abilities related to meeting the identified goals. It is now time to use this information to develop a plan for this unit of instruction.

One way to organize for a unit of instruction is through the use of a unit-planning template. The prompts in each section of the example template provided in table 5.4 are designed to foster the thinking that must occur to successfully differentiate for a diverse group of students.

When completed properly each section of this template will contain specific information. Under the broad heading of learning targets is the prompt for progress indicators. These progress indicators are the identified instructional goals for the unit of study. Typically these progress indicators come directly from the state or district curriculum guides.

In this same broad category are the prompts for what all and some students will know, understand, and be able to do by the end of this unit of instruction. What all students must be able to know and do represents the minimum expectations for students if the teacher is to be satisfied they have mastered the identified progress indicators.

What some students will be able to do is the expectations for those students that have demonstrated the ability to exceed the minimum

Table 5.4. Unit Planning Template

ANYTOWN PUBLIC SCHOOLS UNIT-PLANNING TEMPLATE

Teacher(s): Mr. Jones & Mrs. Smith   **Grade Level:** 5

Subject Area: Language Arts   **Anticipated Length of Unit:** 3–4 weeks

Learning Targets

Progress Indicators:

3.1.1 Students will demonstrate the ability to prepare and deliver a two-to-three-minute oral presentation that includes a clear introduction, main ideas, and a clear conclusion.

3.1.2 Students will demonstrate the ability to deliver a speech using the standard conventions of English, clear articulation, and appropriate voice volume and pace.

3.1.3 Students will demonstrate the ability to use nonverbal elements of delivery to maintain audience interest.

3.1.4 Students will demonstrate awareness of audience members' reactions to the content and delivery of their oral presentations.

3.1.5 Students will demonstrate the ability to ask audience members if they have questions and provide an adequate response to the questions asked.

By the end of this unit of instruction, all students will . . .

Know (facts, vocabulary)	**Understand** (concepts)	Be able to **Do** (skills)
• The parts of a formal speech: introduction, body, and conclusion. • The qualities that define an effective introduction, body, and conclusion. • The qualities that define the effective oral delivery of a formal speech. • The nonverbal behaviors that enhance or detract from the delivery of a formal speech. • The qualities of an effective answer to an audience member's question. • The meaning of the terms: articulation, pronunciation, nonfluencies, voice volume, pace, gestures, and facial expressions	• The relationship between the audience's reactions during the speech and the speaker's need to make modifications during the delivery of the speech. • The relationship between the organization of the speech and the ability of the audience to comprehend the speaker's message. • The relationship between the quality of the speaker's oral delivery and the audience members' ability to comprehend the speaker's message. • The relationship between the speaker's nonverbal behaviors and the audience members' level of engagement.	• Identify an appropriate topic for a two-to-three-minute formal speech. • Write a draft of formal speech topic that includes an introduction, body, and conclusion. • Use proper articulation, pronunciation, voice volume, and pace to effectively deliver a formal speech. • Use posture, eye contact, gestures, and facial expressions to effectively deliver a formal speech. • Identify audience behavior that indicates a need to modify the delivery or content of an oral presentation. • Ask for and then adequately answer audience members' questions.

By the end of this unit of instruction, some students will . . .

Know (facts, vocabulary)	Understand (concepts)	Be able to Do (skills)
• The qualities that make an introduction to a speech engaging. • The qualities that make the body of the speech flow effectively. • The qualities that make the conclusion of the speech most effective.	• Certain qualities of oral delivery and nonverbal behavior enhance the speaker's message.	• Modify the delivery of an oral presentation based on audience members' reactions. • In addition to answering audience members' questions, provide explanations or elaborations that interest the audience.

Learning Experiences

Critical Unit Question(s):
- What makes an oral presentation effective?

Unit Pre-Assessment(s):
- Anytown Speaking Assessment—Prompt 1, assessed via district oral presentation rubric.
- Student journal response to the critical unit question.

Sequenced Topics	*Timeframe*
Parts and basic qualities of an effective oral presentation	2 class periods
Oral delivery of a formal speech	1 class period
Use of nonverbal behaviors when providing a speech	1 class period
Adjusting presentations based on audience reactions	1 class period
Developing drafts of speeches	1 class period
Practicing speeches	1 class period
Delivering speeches and using feedback to improve	2 class periods

Unit Post-Assessment(s):
- Anytown Speaking Assessment—Prompt 2, assessed via district oral presentation rubric.
- Student journal response to the critical unit question.

expectations. In a co-taught class with students that have severe disabilities, this section may also be used to identify the minimum expectations those students will meet if they are deemed to have made sufficient progress.

The first subheading in the Learning Experiences section of the template is for critical unit questions. The purpose of these questions is to drive instruction and assessment for the unit of study. The content of this question or questions must be focused on the key concepts, levels of thinking, and indicators of the skills, process, or demonstration of learning for the final assessment. More specifically, critical unit questions require the deeper levels of thinking necessary to truly demonstrate understanding and proficiency with the standard.

The question in the example unit in table 5.4 is What makes an oral presentation effective? A successful student response to this question will require higher-level thinking built upon a deep understanding of the content presented throughout this unit of study.

Underneath this section of the template is the prompt for the unit pre-assessment. At the end of the template is a section for the post-assessment. A simple description of each assessment is sufficient for these two sections of the template.

The unit post-assessment may differ in form and content but must assess the same knowledge or skills as the pre-assessment. Doing so will allow the teacher to determine and then document student growth over the course of the unit of instruction.

Developing the pre- and post-assessments at the same time is one way to establish this consistency. Also, developing the summative assessment in advance can serve as a powerful guide for instructional decision-making. Teaching to the test is not a problem if the test is a valid, reliable measure of what we truly want students to know and do.

The topics and timeframes column of the template are the space in which "chunks" of the unit are placed. These chunks represent the division of the topic of study into logical sections of learning. To do this, the teachers must understand the necessary sequence of learning that will enable the learner to perform proficiently on the final assessment. A chunk may last for one or multiple class periods. The number of anticipated class periods is listed in the right-hand column.

DEVELOPING LESSON PLANS

When completing the unit plan co-teachers identified and sequenced the topics students must learn in order to meet the goals for the unit of study. Each topic represents a chunk of the learning to be accomplished. These chunks are not the same as daily plans because they may take multiple class periods spread out over the course of multiple days to complete. Table 5.5 is an example of a completed lesson plan.

Table 5.5. Sample Lesson Plan

Anytown USA Lesson Plan

Teacher(s): Mrs. Smith & Mrs. Jones   **Date:** 12/13/2011

Subject Area: Language Arts   **Lesson Title:** Identifying the basic parts of a formal speech.

Learning Target(s): Students will demonstrate the ability to identify the introduction, body, and conclusion in the text of a speech.

Formative Assessment Strategy: Students will be given the text of a short speech. They will use lines and labels to mark the introduction, body, and conclusion sections of this speech.

Lesson Component	Co-Teaching Approach	Time	General Education Teacher	Special Education Teacher	Differentiation and Accommodation Strategies
Activate: Activating relevant prior knowledge and establishing the relevance of learning targets	☐ One lead, one… ☐ Stations ☐ Alternate ☐ Parallel	10 min.	Using Think-Pair-Share format, asks students to recall what they learned about making a speech in 4th grade.	Follows Think-Pair-Share by stating objective for the lesson and asks students to identify their own learning goals.	Prepare Daniel and Jason for the Think-Pair-Share by having them think about an answer in advance.
Acquire: Introducing new knowledge	☐ One lead, one… ☐ Stations ☐ Alternate ☐ Parallel	20 min.	Provides students with the text of several speeches, identifying each major part.	Anticipates student questions, interjecting when appropriate. Highlights the text sections on the overhead.	Provide Daniel, Jason, and Chris with advance copies of the highlighted texts.
Extend: Practicing, reviewing, and applying knowledge	☐ One lead, one… ☐ Stations ☐ Alternate ☐ Parallel	15 min.	Takes Group A and has students practice identifying the three parts of the speech. Provides feedback and correction.	Takes Group B and has students practice identifying the three parts of the speech. Provides feedback and correction.	Group A will have a text that is written at a lower readability level.

The learning target is the driving force that guides every other decision made when completing this plan. The learning target statement includes a description of the content to be learned as well as the cognitive level to be attained by the student. In this case the students are expected to identify the introduction, body, and conclusion in the text of a speech. This is at the understanding level of Bloom's taxonomy.

The next section of this template is the location for describing the method of formative assessment that will be used. The content of this section must relate to the learning target. More specifically, this part of the plan describes the activity students complete in order for their teachers to assess the students' level of understanding of the content presented during the lesson.

The largest section of this lesson plan template contains six columns. The first column, lesson components, describes the three major sections of a learning plan. In the section labeled activate, the teachers' goals are to make sure the students activate relevant prior knowledge, understand the objective for the lesson, and establish reasons for why learning this content is important.

In the section labeled acquire, the teachers' goals are to provide the experiences and models necessary for students to reach the established learning targets. In the section titled extend, the teachers' goals are to provide students with opportunities to practice the learning while receiving corrective feedback. Typically the practice described in this section will gradually move from guided to independent.

Moving horizontally, the next column is the place to check the type of co-teaching approach that will be used for that section of the lesson. Each of the four co-teaching models, as well as how differentiated instruction can be incorporated within that approach, will be discussed in the next chapter.

The time column is simply a place for the teachers to estimate how long it should take to complete the activities in that section. Thinking through this time estimate helps with lesson pacing.

There is a column for the general and the special education teacher. These columns provide a place for the teachers to determine and then describe what their roles and responsibilities will be during that section of the lesson. These descriptions are connected to and elaborate on the instructional model checked off in the co-teaching approach column.

The final column in this section is the place where the teachers will list the necessary differentiation and accommodation strategies they will be using for the students. If there are no accommodations to be made or if no differentiation of instruction will be occurring, this column will be left blank.

UNIT PLAN REFLECTION

An opportunity for continuous improvement is lost when the teachers do not take the time to reflect on the quality of their unit plan. Every unit plan should be considered a work in progress that consistently evolves toward becoming better at meeting students' learning needs. Table 5.6 is an example of a completed checklist co-teachers could use for structured reflection upon completion of an instructional unit.

Working collaboratively, the teachers should decide the degree to which the unit met each criterion. After proceeding through the criteria, teachers should make note of areas that need to be improved for the

Table 5.6. Reflection Form

Anytown Unit Planning Reflection Form			
At the conclusion of your unit of instruction, please rate the degree to which you believe the unit met the following criteria.			
Unit Criteria	Strong	Moderate	Weak
Contained challenging content that required students to use higher-order thinking and problem-solving skills.	X		
Allowed for student choice.	X		
Provided varied activities designed to address different learning styles and preferences.	X		
Provided opportunities for student reflection and self-assessment.		X	
Provided data that could be used to inform and adjust instruction to better meet the needs of varying learners.		X	
Fostered the use of technology as a tool to develop critical thinking, creativity, and innovation skills.			X
The next time this unit is taught we will . . . Find ways to move beyond using the technology simply as a presentation tool. We need to find ways for students to use the available technology to acquire and produce information. We will try to have them create a PowerPoint presentation that will go along with their oral presentations.			

next time they implement this instructional unit. These notes should be kept with the unit so they can be referred to in the future.

PREPARATION OF INSTRUCTIONAL MATERIALS

Despite the push for more authentic tasks, traditional activities like worksheets, answering chapter questions, taking notes, and reading textbooks remain a staple of today's classroom. For many years special education teachers have been making accommodations in general education classrooms for students with individualized education plans required to complete these activities.

The fact that these accommodations are often done poorly or incorrectly frequently makes them a source of confusion and resentment. To effectively use accommodations for preparing instructional materials, teachers must understand and accept some general parameters.

First, teachers must understand the intention behind classroom accommodations. Appropriate classroom accommodations enable students to acquire information and then demonstrate what they know without fundamentally changing the target skills being taught or tested.

Accommodations should not reduce the learning or performance expectations held for students. While they will change the manner or setting in which information is presented or the manner in which students respond, they should not change the target skill or the testing construct. In short, they should not provide an advantage. Instead they simply should "level the playing field."

Second, classroom accommodations are often presented to teachers as long lists of generic practices. To be effective and appropriate most accommodations should be related to the specific demands of the task. Rarely does a student need an accommodation like extended time to complete assignments for every task required in the classroom. An analysis of the demands of the task and the abilities of the students must be the driving force behind the accommodations provided.

Third, classroom accommodations must serve to empower and not humiliate the student. For example, providing a middle school student in a co-taught language arts class with a cartoon version of a novel is likely to lead to the ridicule and embarrassment of that student.

Furthermore, the classroom accommodations implemented should have a neutral to positive impact on the other students' opportunities for learning the content. An adaptation that makes it difficult for other students to learn is not appropriate for a general education classroom.

Most of the accommodations provided to students with individualized educational plans are commonsense representations of good teaching practices. If one looks carefully and thoughtfully at the accommodations required in most IEPs, it becomes obvious that many of these "special education" practices are simply effective means of providing instruction and assessing student learning. Thus, these accommodations are appropriate for many of the students that do not have individualized educational plans.

Keeping these parameters in mind, co-teachers can make many reasonable, doable changes that will help many more students succeed. One such change relates to the importance of quality or quantity of responses required.

If a student can provide quality responses to several questions that require application of the same knowledge or skills, is it necessary for that student to do a large number of those same types of questions? As long as the evens and odds require the application of the same types of knowledge and skills, then perhaps students can do one or the other.

Similarly, not all of the activities or questions within a given worksheet are of equal value. Completion of some of the questions or activities is essential while others may be supplemental. Placing an asterisk by those questions or activities that are essential and then requiring only those be completed is another way to decrease the quantity of responses.

For those concerned about grading this type of activity, satisfactory completion of the asterisked items will earn the grade of a "B." Anyone in the class may select to do all of the items. Satisfactory completion of all of the items on the worksheet shall earn the grade of "A."

If it is important for students to complete all of the problems in a given activity, yet the volume of these problems appears overwhelming to one or more students, the following method of administration may work. In advance of providing the assignment, the activity must be broken into smaller parts. Each of these smaller parts must be able to be administered separately.

As the student finishes one part, he or she raises their hand. One of the teachers then walks over and checks what has been completed. After providing feedback and correction if necessary, that teacher can provide the next section of the worksheet. Ultimately the student does the same amount of work; it is just done in more manageable "chunks."

Teachers often assign students activities, especially certain types of worksheets, that they think will be fun for them to complete. In fact, many students do enjoy word search activities and crossword puzzles. However, these activities are not fun for the students that have difficulty with reading or spelling. Requiring a student with a visual perceptual processing problem to complete a word search activity is cruel and unusual punishment.

When designing classroom materials it often helps to increase the amount of white space surrounding the print. In general, the more white space around the words, the easier it is for the student to read the print.

Eliminating nonessential print is also helpful to increasing reading comprehension. Many classroom activities contain an abundance of words in their directions that are not critical for the completion of the activities.

Questions asked as a part of assignment completion often include vocabulary that is unfamiliar to the students. Frequently this unfamiliar vocabulary is neither integral to the content of the chapter nor has it been the subject of any direct instruction. Students with more extensive reading vocabulary will be at an advantage when faced with this type of situation.

This problem can be alleviated by carefully reviewing the vocabulary required to understand the response sought by the question. Often it is as simple as placing a synonym you are certain the student will know in parentheses above the unfamiliar word. You would not do this if the word was one that had been taught and thus students were expected to know.

Another problem is that questions frequently require more than one response. A simple example is the question, "What is countershading and how does it camouflage fish?" Not only do students have to identify what countershading is, they must also explain how it serves to provide camouflage.

For students with strong language skills understanding the question comes easily. They may not know the answer, but this is not due to struggles with processing the language used to ask the question. On the other hand, a student that struggles with language processing must consciously decode the text.

Because they process the question in segments, answering each segment in isolation, it is very common for these students to complete the first part of the question and then forget to go back and answer the second part. They put an answer down and then do what comes naturally, move on to the next question.

The obvious solution to this problem is simply to divide a multiple-part question into separate questions. Each of the new questions would be placed on a separate line. Taking the example cited above, the two-part question would simply become

"What is countershading?"
"How does countershading camouflage fish?"

Questions frequently provide vague requirements for the expected answer. Questions that ask for "several" or "some" are not precise enough. An example of this type of vague question is "List several characteristics that distinguish sharks from other fish."

Obviously because it says characteristics, this means more than one. Yet, how many characteristics are enough? If the teacher wants the students to name the three ways a shark is different from other fish then that is exactly what the question should state.

If an activity requires the use of a textbook it can be helpful to provide students with cues for finding answers. For example, at the end of the question the page number for locating the answer may be provided in parenthesis. For some students it may even be the page number and paragraph number. Ultimately every student should be taught how to use the parts of a book to locate information. Until that happens some students will intuitively know to use cues from the text while others will start with page one and look through every subsequent page.

Each time you answer a different type of question (i.e., matching, short answer, fill in the blank, etc.) a different reading comprehension strategy is required. Most people are able to switch back and forth with ease. However, for students that require explicit cognitive attention to switch back and forth this type of activity becomes more about reading comprehension than anything else. If at all possible, different types of questions should be grouped together.

Sometimes students need additional scaffolding between guided practice and independent practice. They do not require the assistance of the teacher but they are not quite ready to complete the activities on their own. If the assigned activity requires completion of a series of steps, then the "key ring method" is a potential solution.

For each step in the problem a separate index card is created. Each index card contains a description of the step as well as an example illustrating the completion of that step. These index cards are hole-punched in the corner and then sequentially clipped together on the key ring.

The students will be able to use this series of index cards to prompt them through the successful completion of a multi-step problem. Because it takes more effort to use them, students will not use these key rings if they do not truly need them.

NOTE TAKING

Taking notes from the board or an oral presentation is a common practice that deserves some special attention. This is especially true for middle and high school classrooms. Students that have difficulty with auditory processing or written language production usually struggle with this activity. The most important thing these students can do is focus their attention on comprehending the explanation and examples.

This does not mean that students that struggle with auditory processing and written language production should not take any notes. Instead it means that the teachers should take several steps to change the nature of the lecture while reducing the written output necessary for those students that need this accommodation.

It is not the experience of taking notes that leads to comprehension and retention of content. It is the processing that is done with the content of those notes that leads to increased learning. With this in mind, the following strategies should be applied to improve the note-taking experience for all students.

Just like the example below, have students divide their note page into two columns. At the bottom of the page the students will draw a line across the page large enough to make a box for writing a summary. Provide a partial outline for the students requiring an accommodation for written language or auditory processing difficulties.

The partial outline in this example serves to organize the experience for the students. It also decreases the volume of words that must be written. If necessary this outline could be even more structured by writing phrases with blanks left for students to fill in. For example, "George Washington was the leader of the _____ ____." In this case the student has to listen for and then write the words "Continental Army."

After every five to ten minutes of lecturing (depending upon the age and maturity of students) the teacher will stop. At this point, the students will have two minutes to compare notes with an assigned partner for accuracy.

In addition to making any necessary revisions, they will draw a simple visual in the right-hand column that will help them to remember the most important information presented during that part of the lecture. At the end of the lecture, students will review their notes and write a summary of the content. This may be done in class or for homework.

Executive Branch—President	
A. **Duties**	
1.	
2.	
B. **Departments**	
1.	
2.	
3.	
4.	

This method of note taking requires every student to take notes. Based on need, some students have the note page modified, while others do not. The students with the modified note page still must follow along, but they can focus on content, key concepts, and terms while avoiding feeling the pressure to "get it all down."

Points to Remember

- Instructional planning time is essential if the expectation is that both professionals in the classroom will fulfill active, important roles in the instructional process.
- A structured planning process is vital for effectively using the time provided.
- Planning is a process that begins with determining annual goals, proceeds to unit plans and daily plans, and ends with reflection.
- Advance preparation of instructional materials is frequently necessary in order for students to acquire and demonstrate knowledge and skills.

CHAPTER 6

Instruction in a Co-Taught Classroom

There are four basic models for the delivery of instruction in a collaboratively taught classroom. Each of these models presents unique opportunities for differentiating instructional delivery. The purpose of this chapter will be to describe each model and then make an explicit connection to one or more differentiated instructional methods.

Before proceeding to provide this information, it is important to provide two guidelines for collaborative instruction and a basic overview of the philosophy of differentiated instruction. Regardless of the model of instruction selected, it is important to ensure the roles for working with the various students in the classroom occasionally switch.

If one of the teachers always works with those students requiring additional assistance, the message to students will be that if you need extra help then that teacher is responsible for providing it. This undermines the larger desirable message of shared responsibility for all of the students in the classroom.

The model for delivering instruction selected must be based upon the instructional objectives for the lesson and the needs of the student population. Each of these models has potential for application to various learning activities. However, the activities and models used to deliver them are selected based upon their fit to the lesson objective and student needs, not the other way around.

With that said, it is important to vary your approaches when appropriate and possible. The novelty of using varied models will result in increased student attention to the task. Furthermore, the structure of each model will meet the learning preferences of different students.

The four models to be described in this chapter are structures for the delivery of content to students in a collaboratively taught classroom. Use of these structures is an important step towards capitalizing on having two teachers sharing instruction in one classroom. Yet if both teachers do nothing more than deliver the same content in the same way with the same methods for demonstrating mastery then many students still will find minimal academic success.

In a typical classroom students are at varying levels of readiness to learn the topics being taught. This is primarily due to students' unique experiences and abilities. In addition, students have preferences for how they learn new content and how they demonstrate mastery of this learning. To be successful, co-teachers must acknowledge these facts and then plan differentiated experiences accordingly.

Acknowledging and planning for differences in readiness and learning preferences does not mean provision of a different "watered down" curriculum. Unless a student's individualized educational plan states otherwise, at a minimum every student in the co-taught general education classroom is expected to demonstrate mastery of the general education curriculum standards. This is non-negotiable. However, what is flexible is how students acquire the necessary knowledge and skills and then demonstrate what they have learned.

ONE LEAD, ONE . . .

This model of instruction is the one most frequently used in a collaboratively taught classroom. Perhaps this is because it is the most similar to traditional teaching. In this model, one of the teachers (teacher A) presents the content of the instruction while the other teacher (teacher B) performs various tasks.

There are two advantages associated with this model. One is that it requires minimal instructional planning time. If the teachers do not have any common planning time, at least this is better than one teacher simply wandering aimlessly around the classroom. Second, this model is effective when the most appropriate instructional method is traditional direct instruction. Some content is best delivered in this manner.

There are three cons and a caution associated with this model. First, it is easy to overuse this model. Because it is the most similar to what occurs in a classroom led by one teacher, it is very comfortable. In fact, it may be so comfortable that the co-teachers may not stretch themselves to apply the other models.

Second, the co-teachers may just agree in advance to subdivide the lesson. For example, they may agree that one of them will review the homework and the other will present the lesson. This approach may be labeled "tag-team teaching."

The simple division of lesson responsibilities does not require teachers to collaboratively plan for their instruction. Because of the involvement of two or more professionals with diverse knowledge, collaborative planning usually results in superior instructional plans.

Third, many students do not thrive when presented with information in a traditional manner. The expectation of sitting, listening to the teacher, and perhaps taking notes does not work for students that need a more kinesthetic, interactive experience to learn effectively.

It is easy for this model to turn into competition for "air time." If both teachers are eager to be seen as the lead teacher, those using this approach may speak over one another or consistently interrupt the speech of the other. To be effective, this approach requires proper timing of the vocalizations of each teacher. This is a habit developed based on conscious awareness and experience sharing instruction.

Due to the large group nature of the "one lead and one . . ." model, it presents the fewest opportunities for differentiating instruction. Even so, this model still provides opportunities for the teachers to work collaboratively to meet the needs of their students. While teacher A is providing instruction, teacher B may provide support and assistance by:

- Listening to the presentation of the content and then paraphrasing or elaborating upon what has been said;
- Injecting questions directed toward teacher A based upon anticipation of student misunderstandings;
- Providing on-the-spot visual supplements like graphic organizers or pictures that assist with clarifying the content presented;
- Recording key points on the board or chart paper during lectures or brainstorming activities;

- Operating the technology used to supplement teacher presentations;
- Assisting students with the use of assistive technology devices;
- Using physical proximity to re-direct and maintain the attention of selected students;
- Recording data on student behavior to determine the antecedents, consequences, and frequency of inappropriate behaviors.

STATIONS

In the station teaching approach to instruction the co-teachers plan and provide for instruction at three or more centers located throughout the classroom. The centers may be run by an adult (teacher, volunteer, aide) or independent. When the center is led by an adult, he or she will repeat the content of that instruction to each of the groups as they rotate through that center.

While specific tasks are assigned and an agenda is developed by the teacher, independent centers still provide students with the opportunity to develop, discover, create, and learn a task at their own pace. Often it is necessary and desirable to provide differentiated tasks in the independent centers.

There are four benefits associated with the use of station teaching in a co-taught classroom. First, moving from station to station provides students with the opportunity for physical movement. Too frequently students are required to sit in one place for extended periods of time. Constant sitting results in lethargic behavior and less efficient cognitive processing.

Since the students are subdivided into groups, there will be a smaller student-to-adult ratio at each manned station. This allows for more individualized attention and prompt feedback on performance. It also encourages students to take a more active role in the learning process.

Many classrooms have a limited supply of materials. For example, a classroom may only have a few computers or a limited number of calculators. If this is the case, students can rotate through a station requiring the use of those materials. Materials can be used equitably by each student, even when there are not enough for the whole class.

When common planning time is limited, station teaching is a viable option because it allows for each teacher's planning for the instruction in their own center. However, this can be a problem if both teachers do not account for what will be taught at the other stations.

Other drawbacks include the noise level. Productive noise will be the norm when station teaching is implemented. For students (and teachers) that are sensitive to these auditory distractions this can be a challenge.

Some students do not possess the behavioral skills required to transition from station to station. The movement from one station to the next can be challenging for those that have a difficult time with ending one task and beginning another. In addition, some students do not demonstrate the behavior skills required for completing tasks independently at a center. Just like we need to teach students when to capitalize words or multiply numbers, some of our students will require direct instruction in appropriate behaviors.

The final drawback has to do with the relationship among the activities in the centers. If students are starting at random centers then the teachers must make sure that the content is not sequential.

If you are required to have learned the content at one center in order to perform the tasks at another center, then this progression must be established. Also, if there is a connection between the content of each center then that connection should be made explicit for the students. Commonly the teachers know the connection among the content in the centers, but the students do not.

MENUS

The human brain acts differently when choice is offered. When learners get to choose a task, the resources they can use, or the parameters for accomplishment, their stress levels are lower. In addition they feel more positive about the task and look forward to participating in and hopefully succeeding with task completion. Thus, allowing learners to make appropriate choices should be a regular practice in all classrooms.

One way of offering choice in co-taught classrooms is through choice "menus." Much like a restaurant menu, a classroom menu provides the learner with choices within the parameters established by the teacher.

Teachers may design classroom menus that require the student to complete "must do's" in conjunction with student-selected "choose to do's."

When creating menus it is important to provide choices that represent different ways of interacting with and expressing the content. Gardner's multiple intelligences provide an excellent framework from which to design menu choices. In addition, when providing menu choices it is important that time be spent up front making sure students understand and are familiar with the requirements of each menu activity.

Table 6.1 is an example of a menu designed for spelling practice. Note that this menu requires a combination of must do's and student choices.

Table 6.1. Menu Sample (Both Must Do's and Choices)

Name: _____	Date: _____	Class Period: _____
	WORD BANK	

Select eight spelling words from Lesson Three: Homophones.
Select five different personal spelling words from your personal word log.
Select two of the vocabulary words from chapter 4 of our classroom novel.

Write your fifteen words in the boxes below. Be sure to spell them correctly!

1.	6.	11.
2.	7.	12.
3.	8.	13.
4.	9.	14.
5.	10.	15.

Monday: Write each of the selected words five times on the words-practiced page of your spelling journal.
Tuesday: Find a partner and practice spelling aloud each of the words on your list.
Wednesday: Complete one of the menu activities below. Your choice.
Thursday: Complete a different menu activity. Your choice.
Friday: Spelling test.

Menu Activities		
Write a synonym or antonym for each word.	Divide each spelling word into syllables.	Use magazine cutouts to create a collage of all the words.
Classify your spelling words according to parts of speech.	Alphabetize all of your spelling words.	Write a song or a poem using all of the words.
Write a context sentence for each word.	Write each of your spelling words in cursive two times.	Make a crossword puzzle complete with an answer key.

The next menu example, in table 6.2, does not contain teacher-required must do's. It is simply a set of choices from which students can select the activities they will complete in order to prepare for the upcoming assessment.

Menus are especially effective when they are used for the independent station(s) in the stations model of co-teaching. Because students can select activities that interest them, the teachers are able to provide instruction to the students at the teacher-led instructional stations. Menus are also an excellent choice for assigning students to complete independent practice activities like homework.

PARALLEL TEACHING

The parallel model of teaching requires the co-teachers to divide their students into two relatively equally sized groups. Within these groups, the teachers have three basic options. First, they can teach the same lesson to their respective group. Second, both teachers could teach part of

Table 6.2. Menu Sample (Choices Only)

Name: _____	Date: _____	Class Period: _____

Directions: As we have learned about each region of the United States, you have spent time studying the states. You could probably name half of them by now if you were given a blank map! To learn the others, choose from the following activities. Which ones will help you learn best? Which ones sound the most fun to you? You can repeat an activity more than once. Your goal is to be ready for the test on this subject by next Monday.

Menu Activities		
Label the states on the blank worksheet.	Using the state flashcards, work with a partner to test one another.	Invent a mnemonic to help you remember the names of ten states.
Using magic markers, trace and name each state on a blank map.	Write a poem or story that includes the names of at least ten states.	Add real-life connections (trips, events, historical figures) to all of the states on your map.
Work with a partner to create a song that includes the names of at least ten states.	Create a game that will help you and others learn the names of the states.	Pretend you are taking a vacation from New Jersey to California. Working with a friend, plan your itinerary.

the content and then switch groups. Finally, both teachers could teach the same content but vary their approaches or the level of complexity.

As with the other models, the parallel teaching approach has its strengths and weaknesses. In this model, both teachers are actively engaged in providing instruction. In addition, there is a smaller student-teacher ratio, providing the opportunity for more individualized instruction and attention. Once again, because they are not delivering the entire lesson collaboratively, teachers can plan their own part of the instruction. Less common planning time is required when the parallel model of teaching is used.

Yet the lack of common planning can lead to teachers doing their own thing. As a result the instruction could be inconsistent or even worse, less effective in one of the groups. This is especially likely if the teachers do not share the same level of content knowledge.

Parallel teaching is difficult to do in a confined space. Like stations, there will be productive noise. The competing auditory stimuli could be distracting to both students and teachers. Finally if the teachers plan to switch groups at some point, it can be difficult to manage the timing. Frequently the groups finish at different times.

TIERED ASSIGNMENTS

In general, classroom tasks can require students to demonstrate a range of understanding that begins with the introductory level and ends with a sophisticated level of understanding. There are multiple gradations between these two levels. A simple example that illustrates this progression for the content standard "students will be able to use currency to make change" is:

Introductory: Identify the name and value of each coin
Order the coins according to value
Count coins with mixed values
* *Given a price and payment amount, correctly count change*

Sophisticated: Provide correct change using multiple coin combinations.
* Indicates the grade-level expectation.

Tiering assignments refers to using this continuum of understanding to adjust the complexity of the task. The task itself is based on an identified curriculum objective. Students are pre-assessed and then matched to the appropriate assignment based on their readiness to learn the new material. Data, not categorical label, is the basis for assigning the appropriate activity.

The first step in creating the actual tiered assignment is the creation of an activity clearly focused on demonstrating mastery of the grade-level expectation. Next, the activity is adjusted to provide a more sophisticated level of complexity. Students are then matched to the appropriate assignment. Table 6.3 is an example of a tiered assignment for the following primary school objective: students will identify the main events in a story.

If the level of readiness is approximately equal, then tiering the assignment is especially appropriate for the parallel model of co-teaching. One teacher could work with the group completing the grade-level appropriate assignment while the other works with the group receiving the more advanced assignment. In order to send the appropriate message to students, the teachers must make sure they switch who is assigned to work with each group on a regular basis.

Another approach to systematically differentiating groups in the parallel model of co-teaching is to use different instructional approaches in each group. For example, one of the groups may be instructed via reading the text and then discussing answers to questions with one another.

At the same time, the other group may be watching a video that demonstrates the same content. Students may be assigned to these groups based upon demonstrated preferences for acquiring information. To provide multiple exposures to that content, both groups could switch after completing the first activity.

Table 6.3. Tiered Assignment Example

GRADE LEVEL	Make a four-to-six-panel cartoon strip that shows the sequence of the most important events in this story.
ADVANCED	Choose two events in this story and switch the order in which they occur. Identify the events and explain how this change would impact the ending of this story.

ALTERNATIVE TEACHING

When using the alternative model of teaching, the teachers once again divide the class. However this time the majority of students remain with one of the teachers in a large-group setting. At the same time selected students work in a small group with the other teacher. In this small group the selected students may receive pre-teaching, re-teaching, or other individualized instruction.

It is important that the selection process for the small-group setting be based on need and not label. Any students that require the pre-teaching or re-teaching should be in this group regardless of whether they have an individualized education plan. Of course this requires that the selection process be based on high-quality assessment methods.

Many of the same strengths and drawbacks associated with the other models are found with alternate teaching. There is a smaller student-teacher ratio, resulting in the potential for more individualized instruction and attention. In this model, this individualized instruction is based upon the identified needs unique to the students selected for the small group. As with the other models, this one requires less common planning time because teachers can focus their efforts on developing instruction for their own role in the lesson.

Overuse of this model may result in the development of a "class within a class." If the same students are constantly being placed into the small group for assistance the teachers run the risk of this group taking on a negative connotation. For this reason, it is worthwhile to also use this model to provide enrichment activities. If the majority of the class requires the re-teaching of certain content, then those that have demonstrated mastery should receive enrichment in the small-group setting.

Timing is once again an issue with the use of this model. While the small group is meeting, the larger group should not be learning new content. This would just result in members of the smaller group falling further behind their classmates. Thus, the pre-teaching or re-teaching must take place in the amount of time that the rest of the class is engaged in a different activity.

PRE-TEACHING/RE-TEACHING

Due to either a lack of background knowledge or a lack of prerequisite skills, some students will not be able to effectively acquire the knowledge and skills presented in a given lesson. Without having learned the expected vocabulary and concepts in advance, these students will struggle to comprehend the new material being presented. The solution to this problem is to identify these gaps through pre-assessment and then pre-teach all of the students demonstrating the need for prerequisite content.

One item that often requires pre-teaching is vocabulary words specific to the content. It is important for the comprehension of the material that teachers use research-based strategies to ensure students understand the meaning of these key content-area words. Another student need that can interfere with comprehending new material is gaps in the understanding of concepts that teachers expect students to already know. Sometimes it is necessary to use direct instruction to pre-teach students the background knowledge they are lacking.

Sometimes teachers may assume incorrectly that the learner has the ability to determine how information is organized and related. When students do not see the pattern of information presented or cannot make connections between related items, it is far more difficult to retain the information.

For those students that have difficulty with these cognitive skills pre-teaching through the use of graphic organizers is particularly effective. Once the teachers determine how the information is organized they should use a graphic organizer to make this pattern explicit to the students in advance of the classroom instruction.

Genuine cooperative learning is a valuable instructional strategy in all collaboratively taught classrooms. Yet some students lack the necessary social skills to participate in groups. When this situation exists, pre-teaching these students the necessary social skills will make it possible for them to participate.

Much like we need to provide direct instruction in math or writing, some of our students need explicit instruction in behavior. Direct instruction combined with role-play and feedback can help students learn the group skills necessary for being an effective member of a cooperative learning group.

Pre-teaching is most appropriate for the alternative teaching model of co-teaching. Re-teaching is also primarily used with this model. As educators we must ask ourselves what the message is to students when they receive a failing grade on an assessment and we simply move on to the next topic. If it is important enough to assess, then isn't it important to make sure it has been learned?

After analyzing student performance, teachers place students into two groups. Students in the group that demonstrated sufficient understanding of the content receive enrichment activities designed to extend their understanding. Students in the group that did not demonstrate sufficient understanding receive additional instruction designed to ensure they master the essential content. After receiving this additional instruction these students are assessed again. After this second assessment the class becomes whole again to move on to the next unit of instruction.

Points to Remember

- There are four basic models that can be used for collaborative teaching.
- Each of the four models has strengths and weaknesses.
- The station model of co-teaching is especially well suited to the differentiated instructional practice of menus and contracts.
- The parallel model of co-teaching is especially appropriate for the delivery of tiered assignments.
- The alternative model of co-teaching provides the structure for pre- and re-teaching content.

CHAPTER 7

Continuous Improvement

It takes time and effort to become a high-performing collaborative teaching team. Problems and challenges are inevitable. How these problems are addressed will make a significant difference in the eventual effectiveness of the team. Problems and challenges must be systematically dealt with through effective processes.

Likewise there will be triumphs along the way. Unfortunately, during the process of becoming a high-performing collaborative teaching team, it is easier to focus on what is not working. Occasionally, time must be taken to identify and then celebrate the positive events that occur. These "celebrations" provide the motivation to sustain effort during the more difficult times.

Perhaps the most neglected aspect of collaborative teaching team development is reflection. Team members are so busy dealing with the day-to-day work that there does not seem to be any time for examining team processes. This is an example of dealing with what is urgent instead of what is important. In order to reach their full potential as quickly as possible, teams must reflect on and then improve where necessary the processes they are using.

Reflection, celebration, and problem-solving are three activities collaborative teaching teams must engage in as part of the continuous improvement process. Engaging in these activities will accelerate the teams' growth. Ultimately this will lead to improved results for students and increased satisfaction for the teaching team members.

REFLECTION

As a part of the continuous improvement process, time must be set aside to reflect on the strategies being used by the team. During the first year of working together, team members should set aside an hour every six to nine weeks to complete the following activities. First each team member should read the reflection rubric in table 7.1.

As they are reading this rubric, team members should independently decide which passage most accurately describes their current functioning on each domain. Once both partners finish their ratings they should compare. Where ratings are different, team members should discuss the rationale used for assigning their rating.

Usually some of the ratings demonstrate progress. When this is the case the partners should acknowledge and celebrate their growth. Likewise some of the ratings will reflect lower levels of performance or minimal growth. These ratings are the ones that should be considered for team improvement.

More specifically, team members should decide upon their top priority. They should select the one thing that is most important for moving their team process forward. With this priority established, the team can develop an action plan for improvement in that area. Table 7.2 is a sample of a completed action plan. A blank copy of this template is located in the appendix.

The next time the team meets to reflect on its processes, the initial conversation should be on the results of the previously developed action plan. Goal attainment should be met with celebration, whereas not meeting the goal might indicate the need to conduct problem-solving activities.

PROBLEM-SOLVING

To be done effectively, the process of solving a problem begins with identification of the problem. As simple as this may sound, many teams skip this step. They rush to find solutions that may or may not address the real problem. Thus, to be effective problem-solvers team members

Table 7.1. Reflection Rubric

Collaborative Teaching Team Reflection Rubric

Domain	Proficient	Developing	Beginning
Interpersonal Communication	Our open and honest communication provides our students with a positive model of adult collaboration.	Our communication is interactive but superficial. We avoid potentially productive conflict in an effort to preserve harmony.	Our communication is guarded. We both struggle to correctly interpret one another's verbal and nonverbal messages.
Physical Space	We both move freely around the classroom sharing the appropriate resources and materials.	We share our materials, resources, and classroom space, but it remains clear whose classroom it is.	One of us feels like we are a guest in the classroom.
Student Arrangement	Our students with disabilities are evenly dispersed throughout the classroom. Seating adjustments are made based on instructional activities and student needs.	Students with disabilities are evenly dispersed throughout the classroom.	Regardless of the activity students with disabilities are seated together.
Curriculum Adaptation	Because we believe that students have different learning styles, interests, and readiness levels, we willingly and regularly differentiate the processes used and products required in our classroom.	When appropriate we offer the adaptations made to instructional materials and activities for students with individualized educational plans to other students that could benefit from them.	Adaptations made to instructional materials and activities are limited to those required by students' individualized educational plans.
Instructional Preparation	We both effectively and regularly contribute our knowledge and skills to the development of instructional plans.	We have divided the planning and preparation so that each of us has responsibility for certain tasks.	One of us consistently develops the lesson plan and then shares a copy with the other teacher.

(continued)

Table 7.1. *(Continued)*

Collaborative Teaching Team Reflection Rubric

Domain	Proficient	Developing	Beginning
Instructional Presentation	We use the appropriate co-teaching models to ensure that we are both regularly and purposefully involved in the entire instructional presentation.	The majority of the time one of us is in the role of lead instructor. The other one of us does regularly lead specific classroom activities like reviewing homework.	One of us consistently takes the role of lead teacher while the other takes the role of floating and supporting students.
Classroom Management	We share responsibility for consistently enforcing the agreed-upon classroom rules and routines.	There are mutually agreed expectations for student behavior but our enforcement of these rules regularly differs.	Classroom management is the primary responsibility of one of the teachers. There are no mutually agreed expectations for student behavior.
Student-Teacher Interactions	Our students' behaviors indicate that they see both of us as teachers responsible for the learning of every student in the classroom.	Our students do interact with both of us, but they still demonstrate a tendency to prefer interacting with one of us over the other.	The students with disabilities primarily interact with one of us while the rest of the students primarily interact with the other.
Student Assessment	We are both actively engaged in monitoring and assessing and evaluating the learning of all of the students. Grades for all of the students are mutually agreed upon.	We share responsibility for assessing all student work. We each establish and communicate grades for specific groups of students.	One of us is responsible for assessing the work of the students with disabilities while the other assumes responsibility for assessing the work of the remaining students. Determining grades is the responsibility of one of the teachers.

must take the time to create and agree upon a problem statement prior to brainstorming solutions.

After clearly defining the problem, the team should generate possible solutions. The goal is to brainstorm many alternatives or possible solutions to potentially address the challenge or problem on which the team is focusing. This is a divergent process in which the focus is on generating alternatives, not evaluating them.

Upon completing the brainstorming process, team members move to evaluating each of the options. This is the convergent part of the process, through which the team considers the advantages and disadvantages of each proposed solution. After thoughtful critique of each option, one is selected for implementation. The option selected may also be a modification or combination of several potential solutions.

With a trial solution selected, it is now time to write an action plan. This action plan must include the action to be taken, the person or persons responsible for completing the action, and the deadline for completion. The template for continuous improvement action planning (table 7.2) could also be used to complete this action plan.

Throughout this book it has been mentioned repeatedly that co-teaching is a process that can be learned. There is nothing within these pages that cannot be done by a committed, enthusiastic teacher. However, often the journey is not easy.

Problems and challenges will surface that will discourage even the greatest optimists. Learning new skills may feel awkward and uncomfortable. The hard work and effort required to succeed may result in personal sacrifices. At times you may find yourself wondering if this effort is worthwhile.

During the difficult times try to remember that with patience, persistence, and a positive attitude you will succeed. Others in your situation have found the will and determination necessary. This journey will make you a better a person and a better teacher. It will also provide opportunities for your students far superior to anything they have experienced up to this point in school. At the end of the day when we look at ourselves in the mirror, this is what our vocation is all about. Best of luck!

Table 7.2. Improvement Plan

Collaborative Teaching Team Continuous Improvement Plan

Goal: As a team we will improve our ability to actively engage in monitoring and evaluating the learning of all of our students.

Sequenced Activities	Timeline for Completion	Resources Required	Person(s) Responsible	Evidence of Achievement
Development of a common writing rubric	December 6th	6 Traits writing book	Jane Doe and John Smith	Completed writing rubric
Random, even distribution of final papers	December 13th	Student papers	Jane Doe and John Smith	Even and random stack of papers for each teacher.
Scoring of student papers together to make sure reliability is appropriate.	December 14th	Rubric and a subset of the student work.	Jane Doe and John Smith	Rubric scores are consistent regardless of which teacher evaluates the work.
Independent scoring of student papers.	December 15th	Rubric and assigned student papers.	Jane Doe and John Smith	Rubric score for each student's piece of writing.
Reporting of grades to students. Whole class review with provision of corrective feedback	December 16th	Rubric scores and student papers.	Jane Doe and John Smith	Provision of written and oral feedback to students.

Points to Remember

- Reflection is critical for the long-term growth and development of a collaborative teaching team.
- Problems and challenges are inevitable. It is important to have a systematic, structured process to address these issues.
- Celebration is important for sustaining enthusiasm and energy.

CHAPTER 8

The Role of the Administration

Up until this point the focus of this book has been on the development of teachers' skills as they relate to collaborative teaching. When collaborative teaching does not succeed, frequently school administrators attribute this failure to teachers' actions or attitudes. Conclusions are drawn that the teachers are either unmotivated or unwilling.

While teachers' effort, knowledge, and skill are essential, this assignment of blame is often disproportionate, if not completely inaccurate. Most times when collaborative teaching teams are not operating effectively, it is at least in part due to the fact that there are significant barriers making it difficult or impossible for the team to function.

Educational leaders desiring successful collaborative teaching teams in their schools and districts must create a supportive school context and appropriate performance conditions. They must do this while leaving ample room for collaborative teaching teams to develop their own unique styles and strategies. Achieving this balance requires the administrator to take certain actions, while avoiding others.

The remainder of this chapter will describe four sequential phases, each with a subset of strategies designed to accomplish this goal. These phases may be implemented as part of an initiative to implement collaborative teaching or they may be initiated as a means for improving the current program. Regardless of the starting point, it is important to begin with the first phase—preparing.

PHASE ONE—PREPARING FOR CO-TEACHING

In order to develop effective strategies a collaborative teaching team must know the outcomes expected by those responsible for evaluating the team's work. These outcomes are the answer to the following questions: Why are we implementing collaborative teaching teams? What do we hope to accomplish? Perhaps the goal is improved standardized test scores for students with disabilities. Or maybe the goal is to reduce the number of due process hearings initiated due to claims of least restrictive environment violations.

The outcomes selected will depend upon local needs. Regardless of the content of these desired outcomes, they should require high levels of effort and performance if they are to be achieved. On the other hand they cannot be unrealistic and therefore perceived as impossible to attain.

Furthermore, teams at different levels of development may be expected to achieve different outcomes. Teams at more advanced stages of development can be expected to achieve more challenging outcomes. Just as teachers are expected to differentiate for students at different levels of readiness, administrators can differentiate for co-teaching teams at different stages of development.

While it is important to specify the desired outcomes, it is equally important to avoid specifying the details of the processes to be used. Within established boundaries teams must have the freedom to develop and implement their own performance strategies. This is vital for the motivation required to complete the tasks as well as for the ownership of the team's accountability.

Step One—*Establish a challenging and clear purpose for collaborative teaching in your school or district.*

With clarity regarding the tasks to be achieved, it becomes much simpler to assign the correct personnel. Frequently administrators look for volunteers for collaborative teaching. This is a mistake. First, the composition of teams is too important to be decided in this manner. Second, making it voluntary sends the wrong message to staff. The composition of the classes taught and the willingness to collaborate should not be viewed as optional.

So how does one select teachers for collaborative teaching assignments? With a staff roster in hand, the first step is to determine which of your staff members have basic levels of interpersonal skills, task-specific knowledge, and a personal teaching efficacy. Basic, not necessarily exemplary, interpersonal skills are essential. The teacher must have enough interpersonal and social skills that their lack will not interfere with task completion.

The task-specific knowledge required for collaborative teaching includes mastery of differentiated instruction and assessment practices. Knowledge of and experience with instructional models that require peer support (peer tutoring, cooperative learning) is also valuable. A teacher that enters into collaborative teaching with this knowledge and these skills will be more likely to design lessons that meet a wide variety of students' needs.

Of the three criteria mentioned, personal teaching efficacy is perhaps the most important. Personal teaching efficacy is the teacher's sense of personal responsibility for meeting the needs of all students. Teachers with a high degree of personal teaching efficacy take it as a professional challenge to do whatever is necessary to ensure all of the students achieve success.

Step Two—*Develop a list of all of the staff members that meet the criteria of having basic levels of interpersonal skills, task-specific knowledge, and a high degree of personal teaching efficacy.*

With a list of potential teachers to assign, it is now time to compose teams. When composing collaborative teaching teams the goal is to strive for a moderate level of diversity between the members. In other words the aim is to find an appropriate balance between the teachers' similarities and differences.

The strength of a team is partially attributable to the fact that members bring different knowledge, skills, viewpoints, beliefs, values, attitudes, etc. This is what makes it possible for them to do more together than they could accomplish on their own.

However, when the diversity is too great it becomes difficult for team members to understand and relate to one another. For example, placing a special education teacher who strongly believes in systematic phonics instruction in a collaboratively taught classroom with a language arts teacher that is a whole language advocate is likely to be problematic. These two teachers' philosophies of instruction are so different it would be difficult for them to find and utilize common instructional strategies.

Step Three—*Match the teachers from the list created in step two in order to achieve a balance between their similarities and differences.*

Creating teams composed of a balanced mix of personnel, each of which has the appropriate knowledge, skills, and attitude, is critical. However, for teams to reach their full potential a schedule supportive of collaborative teaching is necessary. When developing the schedules for collaborative teaching teams, the responsible administrator must select models based upon student needs, as identified in the individual educational plans, and the possible personnel.

Working within these parameters there are at least four options. The first scheduling option is to have the special education teacher divide his or her time between two different classes based on the activities being conducted and the needs of the student. A second option is to have the special education teacher co-teach in different classrooms on different days. A third option is to have the special education teacher serve as a resource for a team of general education teachers, who then identify and schedule essential opportunities for student support on a weekly basis. Lastly, a team of teacher assistants can be assigned to a special education teacher, who then is given the responsibility for supporting a caseload of students with disabilities.

Another aspect of scheduling that must be considered is the provision of common planning time. Without adequate, regular common planning time collaborative teaching teams do not capitalize on the respective knowledge and skills of each of the team members. Typically the special education teacher takes the role of "floating and supporting" the students because he or she did not have any role in developing the instructional plan.

Common planning time is not a resource easily acquired. Creative options may need to be considered. The first of four options to consider is building into the school calendar periodic early release days. When the students go home early, the teachers can stay and plan together.

A second option is to allot portions of regularly scheduled faculty meeting time to collaborative planning. Given how teachers normally feel about faculty meetings, this option may be especially popular. Another possibility is to combine classes for a period to free up a teacher's time. This may work when the students are doing an activity like watching a video, reading silently, or attending a presentation by a guest speaker. Lastly, substitute teachers can be hired to rotate in pairs among classes. Having the substitute for a class period allows the teachers in that class the opportunity to plan for instruction.

Step Four—*Develop schedules that include common planning time, meet student needs, and utilize personnel resources effectively.*

The final step to be completed by the administrator prior to initially meeting with the collaborative teaching teams is creation of classroom rosters. Sometimes administrators create classroom rosters in which all of the students that could use extra assistance, but do not qualify for it, are placed in collaboratively taught classrooms. While well-intentioned, this action does not result in a heterogeneous group. As a result, student needs are overwhelming and teacher frustration or burnout become distinct possibilities.

Another scheduling mistake is to view all students with disabilities equally. Anyone that has taught students with special needs understands that a student with a significant behavioral disability requires far more attention and support than a student with a mild learning disability. The severity and nature of a student's disability must be considered when developing a class roster.

Strategically clustering students based on the level of support anticipated is one means for achieving this goal. This clustering requires assigning a numerical value to each student. For example, students with minor academic needs are assigned the value of "1." Students with moderate learning or behavioral needs count as "2." Students with significant needs count as "3." By weighting students based on anticipated needs and then striving to achieve equal totals across class rosters, the administrator is more likely to develop a manageable class list.

Step Five—*Create classroom rosters that are heterogeneous and realistic based on students' needs.*

PHASE 2—LAUNCHING CO-TEACHING

Having completed the first five steps, it is time to initiate the collaborative teaching process with the teaching team members. This is the single greatest opportunity for an administrator to have an impact on the eventual trajectory a collaborative teaching team will take.

Teams are the most receptive to intervention at this point in the process. Furthermore, teams that have a strong start have a high probability of achieving long-term success. Teams that start negatively usually do not recover. Beginnings are too important to leave to chance!

Bearing in mind the importance of a strong beginning, collaborative teaching teams should receive team-based, high-quality training prior to their work with students. More specifically, the teaching team members should simultaneously attend professional development provided by a knowledgeable presenter before working with students.

The content of this training must facilitate a successful start for the teams. Essential training topics include:

- Getting acquainted;
- Defining team teaching and its benefits for teachers and students;
- Establishing team parameters and mutual goals;
- Developing rules, routines, academic expectations, and responsibilities;
- Discussing models of collaborative teaching and planning;
- Accessing available district resources;
- Viewing collaborative teaching as a developmental process.

Materials and descriptions for each of these topics have been covered throughout the previous chapters in this book. For specifics on how to implement this content through a workshop format see *Leading Effective Meetings, Teams and Work Groups in Districts and Schools* (Jennings, 2007).

Step Six—*Provide high-quality, team-based training on essential content prior to expecting the teachers to work collaboratively with their students.*

The second major task to be completed in the very early stages of collaborative teaching involves communicating expectations, setting boundaries, and establishing protocols for the flow of information. The expectations you will communicate are the outcomes developed in step one of the first phase. These must not only be shared, they must also be understood.

To be creative and adaptive, collaborative teaching teams must be encouraged to exercise authority to select and manage their own performance strategies. In other words, within the parameters of the student's IEPs and school and district policies a team must have the ability to determine the processes it will use to meet the established expectations.

Freedom within boundaries is essential for motivation and ownership. Thus, either as part of the initial training or at another time very early in the process, team members must be informed of the boundaries they should operate within. For example, common planning time will be used for common planning of instruction. They must also understand that they have freedom to operate within these boundaries.

Frequently students with disabilities receive services from many different staff members. For example, they may receive speech and language therapy or counseling from a school psychologist. When multiple parties are working with a specific student, it becomes difficult to ensure communication is current and accurate.

For example, a parent shares information with a speech therapist and assumes the therapist will communicate with the classroom teacher. When this communication does not occur, the parent begins to question the credibility and competence of the school personnel.

Situations such as these can be avoided by developing protocols for sharing information between related service providers and collaborative teaching team members. Once expectations for what will be communicated and protocols for how this communication will occur are established, the flow of information improves.

Step Seven—*Early in the process communicate expectations, establish boundaries, and develop protocols for what and how information will be shared among those working with the students.*

PHASE THREE—SUSTAINING CO-TEACHING

The most influence a school administrator can have on the long-term development of a collaborative teaching team partnership comes from the implementation of the decisions made in the first phase, during phase two. However, this does not mean the administrator plays no role in the team's continued development.

Through their actions, school administrators can facilitate the continued growth and development of collaborative teaching teams. In other words, they can sustain the momentum initiated when the activities from the previous phase are concluded. There are four actions school administrators should take to achieve this goal.

First, the school administrator must regularly provide structured opportunities for teams to celebrate, reflect, and problem-solve. If these activities are not structured and facilitated they will give way to the demands of daily work. In order for continued long-term growth to occur, this cannot happen.

Celebration provides the opportunity to focus on what is going well. Early on, finding those things that are working and paying attention to them is critical for sustaining motivation. Reflection provides the opportunity to think about, discuss, and plan for improvements in the team processes. Guided problem-solving activities provide support for dealing with the inevitable issues that will serve as obstacles if left unaddressed.

Many types of activities can be used to accomplish these three goals. Regardless of the nature of the activities used, it is important to make sure these activities are not perceived as a burden. They should occur at a time other than the end of the school day and in place of another responsibility.

Step Eight—*Provide structured opportunities on a regular basis for teams to celebrate, reflect, and problem-solve.*

The earliest phases of collaborative teaching are usually stressful for teachers. To help the teachers deal with the anxiety and discomfort they may be experiencing, it is critical to "sustain their hearts." Support provided via positive recognition provides hope and maintains the will to persevere.

Thus, the second action a school administrator can take to sustain a team's momentum is to regularly conduct walk-through observations focused on highlighting the positive aspects of the collaborative teaching situation.

More specifically, on a frequent basis the school administrator should visit the collaboratively taught classroom. During these visits he or she should focus on finding a concrete, specific, and positive aspect of the collaborative teaching situation. Following the walk-through visit, honest feedback on what was observed should be provided either orally or in writing.

Step Nine—*Regularly conduct walk-through observations focused on providing feedback to the teachers on the positive aspects of the co-teaching situation.*

School-level administrators can make or break the success of collaborative teaching teams. Through their language and interactions, school leaders shape and sustain school culture. For collaborative teaching to thrive, this culture must be characterized by norms of acceptance for individual differences as well as an emphasis on the things that those with disabilities can do. Specific actions school-level administrators can take to promote these cultural norms include:

- Use person-first language when referring to the students. For example, "Jason is a student that has a learning disability."
- In your disciplinary actions and conversations with teachers, model determination, persistence, and ownership for all your school's students.
- Proactively address with teachers, parents, and students misconceptions regarding fairness. Fairness is not giving everyone the same thing. It is doing your best to give everyone what they need with the resources available.

- Avoid the use of nicknames (i.e., the inclusion class, special education class) when referring to collaboratively taught classrooms. These labels stigmatize the class.
- Do not allow teachers to choose to teach collaboratively. Working collaboratively should be an expectation for all teachers.
- Do not allow parents to choose whether to have students in collaboratively taught classrooms. Would you allow these same parents to decide whether they want their child in a classroom with students of a different ethnicity or religion? Of course not—disability, like other demographic characteristics, is part of the variation among students found in public schools.
- Do not regularly pull the special education teacher to cover other duties. How important is that teacher to the operation of the classroom if he or she is consistently being reassigned elsewhere?

Step Ten—*Through their words and actions, school-level administrators must shape and sustain a school culture that promotes acceptance and high expectations for all.*

It is common for collaborative teaching teams to experience difficulties. Usually these difficulties are caused by a deficiency in one or more of the following four areas: lack of effort; lack of knowledge or skill; poor implementation of performance strategies; insufficient material resources.

The administrator responsible for helping the teachers work through their difficulties must use observation and discussion to systematically diagnose the source of the problem. Once the source of the problem has been identified, appropriate interventions can be developed. For example, if observation and discussion reveal that the teachers are not correctly using the collaborative teaching models described in the training program (a poor implementation of performance strategies), then an intervention can be targeted to address that specific concern.

Although it should be done with extreme caution, there comes a point at which a team is displaying such dysfunctional behavior that it must be broken apart. This point is either when the team's behavior is consistently having a negative impact on student learning or when team members' interactions are repeatedly poor models of adult behavior for students.

When necessary, additional professional development may be the solution. Frequently, patience and an understanding of the developmental nature of the process are all that is necessary. Sometimes the school administrator needs to remain calm enough for everyone.

However, if the time comes to make the split, it is important for the responsible administrator to discuss the situation with all of the teaching team members present. In this conversation it must be made clear that the split is in the best interest of the students and the expectation for teacher collaboration remains intact.

Step Eleven—*Use observation and discussion to systematically diagnose and then develop targeted interventions for collaborative teaching team difficulties.*

PHASE FOUR—EVALUATING AND IMPROVING CO-TEACHING

Evaluation of co-teaching is necessary for sustained and continuous improvement. Doing this evaluation correctly requires the collection and analysis of both formative and summative data. The data collected should provide answers to the following three questions.

First, does the productive output of the collaborative teaching team meet or exceed the performance standards established by school and district leadership? In other words, are the outcomes resulting from the team's efforts equal to or greater than the outcomes expected? These outcomes were established in phase one and communicated to team members during phase two.

Question two: Have the social processes used in collaboratively teaching maintained or enhanced the capacity of those co-teaching to work together on subsequent tasks? One of the overarching goals for collaborative teaching is the continuous improvement of adult collaboration. If the social processes used by the team members do not maintain or improve this capacity then this goal has not been achieved.

The final question: Does the experience of collaborative teaching satisfy more than it frustrates the personal needs of the team members? Even if the desired outcomes are achieved and the social processes are effective, it would be difficult to say that co-teaching is a success if one or more of the team members' experiences were so negative they do not wish to continue.

One means of providing feedback to teachers is through the traditional classroom observation process. Most observation tools and templates do not work for collaborative teaching situations. They have been designed to provide feedback to teachers working in isolation.

It may be necessary to design a new tool or revise one of the existing ones in order to focus on the key instructional components of the co-teaching model. Regardless of the forms used, to be of value the process must result in providing teachers with meaningful feedback they can use to improve co-teaching.

Lastly, collaborative analysis of data that leads to action planning frequently reveals the need for additional outside expertise. For example, data analysis and action planning may reveal that teams do not know how to assess and plan for reducing disruptive student behaviors. If no one on staff has this expertise, then the educational leader is responsible for acquiring the necessary resources for the collaborative teaching teams.

Step Twelve—*In order to achieve continuous improvements in co-teaching, administrators must use the right balance of tools to assess and evaluate the social processes used, personal satisfaction obtained, and outputs produced by the co-teaching teams.*

Every school administration certificate or license should have a warning reading "Caution—change leadership can be dangerous to your personal health and professional longevity." Leading changes in the delivery of special education toward the model described in this book is one such risk.

There will be times, especially early on, when colleagues, teachers, parents, and maybe even students will question the wisdom of this approach to special education service delivery. If you truly believe this model will yield positive outcomes for staff and students, then this is the time you must have the will and the courage to stay the course.

If you can follow the principles outlined in this chapter and are willing to persist when others around you lose faith, then you will have taken a major step toward leaping the abyss of failure that has plagued the provision of special education for too long. May your journey be both successful and fulfilling.

Points to Remember

- Administrators establish the conditions necessary for increasing the probability teachers will succeed with collaborative teaching.
- The actions administrators can take to increase the likelihood of successful collaborative teaching can be divided into four sequential phases. Each phase has specific actions to be completed by administrators.
- Despite the best-laid plans, sometimes it becomes a test of will and courage to successfully lead this type of change.

Appendix

Collaborative Teaching Team's Goal-Setting Template

Baseline Data

Goal Statement

Strategies

Outcome

IEP SUMMARY SHEET

Case Manager: **Student's Name:**

This student has a disability and must receive specialized instruction, accommodations, modifications, and related services in accordance with his/her Individualized Educational Program. All teachers providing instruction and services for students with disabilities must be aware of the student's needs. The following information is confidential and must be kept in a secure location.

<u>Student(s) Strengths, Interests, and Preferences:</u>

<u>Student(s) Challenges:</u>

<u>Additional Relevant Information:</u>

Please see me if you have any other questions/concerns about this student. I will be his case manager for this year. I look forward to working with you to make sure this year is a positive experience for all of us. My contact information is:

Phone Number: **E-Mail:**

Case Management and Related Services Providers

Student Initials	Case Manager	Speech			Occupational Therapy			Physical Therapy			Counseling		
		Required	Day(s)	Time	Required	Day(s)	Time	Required	Day(s)	Time	Required	Day(s)	Time

Accomodations at a Glance

Student Initials	Extra Time on Tests	Extra Time on Assignments	Textbooks on Tape	Reduce Number of Problems	Test in Small Group	Present Material Orally and in Writing	Oral and Written Directions	Fewer Items Per Page	Enlarge Page	Provide Study Guides	Do Not Penalize for Spelling Errors	Other

MEETING LOG			
Date:	**Start Time:** _____		**End Time:** _____
AGENDA			
Items:			**Time Limit**
1.			
2.			
3.			
4.			
5.			
ACTION PLAN			
Action Items		**Person Responsible**	**By When?**
1.			
2.			
3.			
AGENDA FOR NEXT MEETING			
Date: _____	**Time:** _____		**Location:** _____
Expected Topics:			
1.			
2.			
3.			

Annual Instructional Guide	
Subject Area:	Grade Level:
Teachers:	
Unit Title	*Anticipated Pacing*

Collaborative Teaching Team Continuous Improvement Plan				
Goal:				
Sequenced Activities	*Timeline for Completion*	*Resources Required*	*Person(s) Responsible*	*Evidence of Achievement*

References

Guzzo, R.A. & Dickson, M.W. (1996). Teams in organizations: Recent research on performance and effectiveness. *Annual Review of Psychology*, 47, 307–338.

Hollowood, T.M., Salisbury, C.L., Rainforth, B., & Palombaro, M. (1995). Use of instructional time in classrooms servicing students with and without severe disabilities. *Exceptional Children*, 61, 242–253.

Hunt, P., Staub, D., Alwell, M. & Goetz, L. (1994). Achievement of all students within the context of cooperative learning groups. *Journal of the Association for Persons with Severe Handicaps*, 19, 290–301.

Jennings, M.J. (2007). *Leading Effective Meetings, Teams and Work Groups in Districts and Schools.* Alexandria, VA: Association for Supervision and Curriculum Development.

Levi, D. (2007). *Group Dynamics for Teams.* Thousand Oaks, CA: Sage Publishing.

Sharpe, M.N., York, J.L., & Knight, J. (1994). Effects of inclusion on the academic performance of classmates without disabilities. *Remedial and Special Education*, 15, 281–287.

About the Author

Matthew J. Jennings is currently the superintendent of schools for the Alexandria Township Public School System. Prior to serving in this position, Dr. Jennings served as an assistant superintendent of schools, a director of student services, a supervisor of curriculum and instruction, and a classroom teacher. He earned his master's degree and doctorate in educational administration from Rutgers University.

In addition to presenting at numerous state and national conferences, Dr. Jennings has served as an organizational behavior consultant to school districts throughout New Jersey. His work has been published in *Kappan, Preventing School Failure*, the *New Jersey English Journal, Channels*, and *The Writing Teacher*. His most recent publication, *From the Classroom to the Office: The School Administrator's Guide to a Successful First Year*, was released by Rowman and Littlefield Education in December of 2009.

When he is not spending time with his wife MaryAnn, his children Ryan and Tara, and their dog Amber, Dr. Jennings enjoys time at the beach, competing in triathlons, and Rutgers football games.

www.ingramcontent.com/pod-product-compliance
Lightning Source LLC
Chambersburg PA
CBHW051529230426
43668CB00012B/1786